AF604080

OBEDIENCE FOR A PAYCHECK

DR. CRYSTAL HERNANDEZ

chpsyd@gmail.com | drcrystalhernandezllc.com

Published by Argyle Fox Publishing | argylefoxpublishing.com
Publisher holds no responsibility for content of this work.
Content is the sole responsibility of the author.

First Edition
ISBN 979-8-89124-170-1 (Paperback)
ISBN 979-8-89124-110-7 (Hardcover)

ARGYLE FOX
PUBLISHING

TABLE OF CONTENTS

DEDICATION

This book is written for those who have felt something wasn't right but couldn't quite name it.

For those who showed up every day, did the work, and quietly carried the weight of environments and employers that asked for more than they ever gave back.

For those who have been overlooked, silenced, questioned, or made to feel like their voice, their instincts, or their worth were somehow less than.

This is for the ones who stayed and learned how to survive in systems that slowly asked them to shrink.

For the ones who aligned—not because they lacked integrity, but because they were trying to succeed, belong, and build a life.

For the ones who did not realize, at first, that what they were adapting to was not just culture, but conditioning.

And this is for those who resisted. The ones who asked the questions. Who saw clearly when others could not—or would not. Who stepped out onto that ledge, knowing the ground beneath them might disappear. You took the risk. You carried the weight. You felt the isolation. And you did it anyway.

There are people still inside these systems navigating, surviving, enduring—often in silence.

There are people who have been pushed out of the systems who are now trying to rebuild, repair, and reclaim who they are.

And there are people still trying to make sense of what they experienced.

This book is for all of you, because what you felt was real. What you saw was valid. And what you carried was never yours alone to hold.

INTRODUCTION

Organizations should not be something you merely survive. Yet for many professionals, that is exactly what they become.

Fortunately, many workplaces are healthy.

I've worked in environments that were thriving—where culture was supportive, where people felt valued, where showing up to work felt purposeful. In these places, collaboration was real, leadership made decisions that aligned with the organization's values, and I left at the end of the day feeling productive, respected, and wanted.

But that's not the focus of this book. *Obedience for a Paycheck* looks at unpleasant work environments, the businesses you warn friends about. I've experienced them firsthand.

The culture in such environments goes beyond difficult. It can be deeply damaging. Gaslighting blurs reality, intentional siloing limits access and understanding, and isolation is a tool. Retaliation—sometimes subtle, sometimes direct—follows those who question, challenge, or see too clearly.

If you've only experienced one or the other, rest assured both experiences are real. Both exist, often within the same profession, the same sector, and sometimes even the same organization over time.

Despite what HR or upper management may claim, our human experience is exactly that—our experience.

What we feel is valid.

What we experience is real.

And how we process, understand, and ultimately heal from those experiences is not fixed. It's a unique process for each individual that promises limitless possibilities for those willing to do the critical work.

Recognizing such a toxic organization can be difficult. What begins as meaningful work of service, purpose, and mission slowly shifts into something harder to name. The language often stays the same, but the experience changes. Something feels off, but it's hard to put a finger on it.

New rules show up, unwritten but rigid.

Expectations expand, implied but enforced.

Loyalty and value to the company are measured not by performance but by silent devotion.

Questions are noticed. Patterns are ignored. Over time, a once-beloved workplace morphs into something else entirely, a distorted caricature.

In these environments, people adapt. Some internalize the system completely. They convince themselves all is well and come to believe in it, defend it, and reinforce it. Sometimes, they do this without realizing a dramatic shift has taken place and all is not well.

Others learn to exist within the new system. They keep their heads down, adjust their expectations, and trade opportunity and joy for stability. Neither fully accepted nor openly rejected by those who masterminded the transition, these cogs simply remain in place until their use runs out.

Then there are those who resist. They ask questions, document, and challenge. They push against decisions that don't make immediate sense or clash with the organization's stated values, those values that kept the organization moving forward throughout its history. For their efforts, these resisters often pay dearly.

This book is about these systems—how they form, how they're sustained, and what they do to the people inside them.

But it is also about something more important: choice. Because whether consciously or not, every person inside these environments is navigating one of three paths.

1. To survive by adapting
2. To submit by assimilating
3. Or to speak and risk everything

Modern organizations across sectors can develop dynamics that are not just unhealthy, but also structurally controlling. These environments are not accidental. They're reinforced by leadership structures, incentives, and cultural norms that reward compliance and discourage dissent. Over time, these organizations begin to shape behavior, belief, perception, and identity.

And within these systems, people adapt in predictable ways: assimilation, marginal survival, or resistance.

This is not theoretical for me. I've worked inside these systems. I've observed them across sectors. I've lived through the phases of adaptation—at times avoiding conflict, staying quiet, and learning where the lines were in order to protect my job and mental stability.

Stepping forward and questioning forced me to stand in spaces that felt uncertain, exposed, and at times very isolating. Sadly, this experience is exceptionally common. Over the years, I've seen what happens when people stay silent, and I've seen what happens when they don't.

The Three Survival Paths Model™

Every reader within one of these beyond-toxic work environments should see themselves within this framework.

1. Assimilate (The Indoctrinated)

- Internalize organizational beliefs
- Protect leadership and culture
- Reinforce the system (knowingly or unknowingly)

2. **Exist (The Fringe Survivors)**
   - Stay under the radar
   - Minimize harm and visibility
   - Trade growth for psychological safety
3. **Resist (The Disruptors)**
   - Question, challenge, and document
   - Raise concerns internally or externally
   - Apply pressure that may create disruption
   - In some cases, escalate to whistleblowing

This framework is not about judgment. It is about understanding. Because once you understand how these systems operate and how people adapt within them, you gain something powerful. Clarity. And with clarity comes the ability to decide how to navigate the system. More importantly, you're empowered to choose who you want to be within that system or whether you should leap through the nearest escape hatch.

OBEDIENCE
FOR A
PAYCHECK

Chapter 1

THIS ISN'T JUST TOXIC—IT'S STRUCTURED

ANYONE WHO SPENDS ENOUGH TIME in these environments becomes a professional. They're so good at what they do, it takes time to see how their deformity mirrors their environment, because these professionals wear a mask all day, every day, and most environments don't begin as beacons of treachery.

The Honeymoon Phase

When you first enter an organization, there is often a sense of possibility. The mission feels meaningful, the people seem aligned, and the work feels purposeful. You want to be there.

I've experienced these environments, where cultures were thriving, supportive, and grounded in genuine collaboration. Places where I felt valued. Where showing up to work felt energizing. Where I left at the end of the day feeling productive, purposeful, and wanted.

In these spaces, work isn't something to endure. It feels like something to build. But not all environments stay that way, and not all environments reveal themselves immediately.

That's what makes these organizations so difficult to navigate and even harder to name. The clarity of a system is rarely visible during this phase, and that's what makes it so effective at deception.

When Something Begins to Shift

At some point—often quietly—something changes. The change isn't substantial enough to clearly define or immediately act on. It's just enough to notice, to raise an eyebrow or two.

It may look like a decision that doesn't align with stated values, a leader whose message shifts depending on the audience, or a colleague who becomes less visible and less included, without explanation.

These moments are subtle, and because of their subtlety, they're easy to rationalize. After all, every organization has challenges, every leader has blind spots, and every system has complexity—right?

I told myself those same things. Because early on, it's difficult to distinguish between normal organizational friction and something more structured beginning to take shape.

The Moment You Don't Trust Yet

Early in my career, I listened in on a meeting as a decision was made that clearly misaligned with what was communicated publicly. The decision wasn't dramatic. There were no raised voices or overt disagreement. But there was a pause—so brief it was almost imperceptible.

People around the table looked at each other and nodded, then moved on.

Maybe I'm missing something, I thought. There must be more context. And I kept my thoughts to myself.

Looking back, that moment of unease wasn't about the decision. It was about what didn't happen. It was about the fact that no one asked, clarified, or challenged the incongruous decision. I now see that the silence in the room was not accidental. It was learned.

Why It's Hard to See Clearly

Part of the difficulty in seeing clearly is timing.

When you enter one of these organizations, you're new. You're learning, trying to understand how things work. So, you do what comes naturally to new people. You observe before questioning, adapt before challenging, and assume there's context you don't yet understand.

In the past, these steps have saved you embarrassment and kept you from sticking your foot in your mouth. Unfortunately, these same steps can also begin the slow process of indoctrination. Because sometimes, what you see isn't confusion. It is signal.

The problem is that early signals are rarely strong enough to fully trust. So instead of naming them, you adjust around them. The adjustments are incremental—so incremental you don't realize what's happening.

The Language We Use and Why It Falls Short

When something feels off at work, people often use one word: toxic. The word captures discomfort, frustration, and sometimes harm. Strong as the word is, it softens what is actually happening.

Toxic suggests something vague, something diffuse and unintentional. Something that simply exists. But what I have experienced and what many professionals experience isn't vague. It is patterned, reinforced. Over time, it becomes structured.

From Culture to Control

Healthy organizational culture is built on shared values, accountability, and the ability to question and improve. In some environments, culture shifts. The shift is never abrupt and rarely formal. It happens slowly but surely through repetition, response, and reinforcement. It moves from something that guides behavior to something that begins to control it.

This shift is not always intentional. It can emerge from inside or outside pressure, leadership dynamics, or the need to maintain a specific image or stability. It can even come from incentive structures that reward compliance over integrity.

No matter the root cause, intent does not prevent impact. And impact—not intent—shapes the system.

I've seen this shift happen across organizations, and I have lived inside it. At times, I adapted and stayed quiet. I navigated carefully because the risk of doing otherwise felt too high. At other times, I saw the shift clearly, and it was impossible to ignore.

What the System Teaches

In these environments, the most important rules aren't written. They're learned through observation, experience, and consequence. After all, the system does not need to explain itself.

Inside the system, you learn without being taught. Lessons you learn include:

- Which questions are safe and which are not
- Which concerns are welcomed and which are quietly dismissed
- Which behaviors lead to opportunity and which lead to exclusion

No one gives these lessons directly. There is no PowerPoint presentation during a weekly or quarterly meeting with shareholders. But the system makes itself unmistakably clear.

The Quiet Consequence

A highly capable, thoughtful, and respected colleague once asked a reasonable question during a team discussion. The question wasn't confrontational or even disruptive. In fact, the question was appropriate and necessary.

The response, on the other hand, was neutral—at least in the moment. Management acknowledged the question, redirected the conversation, and moved onward.

In the weeks that followed, my colleague and I realized the response to the question was not neutral. Something changed. My colleague was excluded from certain conversations. Opportunities that should have come her way were sent elsewhere. Even the tone used toward her changed. None of this was overt enough to formally address, but it was obvious enough for anyone paying attention to see.

That was the point. The system didn't need to say what happens when questioned. It gave the answer in more tangible ways.

The Gap You Can Feel

One defining feature of these systems is the gap between what is said and what's experienced. As organizations move toward a structured toxicity, administrators continue to use the right language. Their words are mission-driven, values-based, and integrity-focused.

On the surface, everything appears aligned. But internally, the experience begins to feel different. Decisions contradict values. Outcomes reward alignment over effectiveness. Behavior is shaped more by loyalty than truth.

These shifts create tension as you realize you're told one thing while experiencing another.

Why It's So Difficult to Name

While the experience is real, it's difficult to articulate. That's because these systems are not defined by overt control. They're ruled by subtle reinforcement.

There are no explicit rules set forth demanding loyalty. You wont' find formal policies that discourage dissent. Instead, behavior gets shaped indirectly through access, inclusion and exclusion, and tone, timing, and response.

There is no single moment to point to, no inflection point at which everything changed. There are only patterns. And patterns are inherently harder to prove—especially when each moment can be explained away in isolation.

This Is Not About Individual Personalities

A good-natured person can easily attribute these difficult, squirm-inducing dynamics to something innocuous. Perhaps the problem is caused by a bad leader, a difficult colleague, or a single poor decision. Perhaps. Then again, I've seen these patterns repeat across organizations in different sectors under different leadership with wildly different missions.

When such a pattern repeats across systems, it ceases to be an individual problem and becomes structural, the very thing holding an organization upright.

From Toxic to Indoctrination

Not every difficult workplace is structured. However, when patterns become consistent, behavior is shaped predictably, and individuals must adjust what they do and how they think, the system has shifted.

At this point, it's no longer just a difficult workplace. It's a workplace with a harmful, structured backbone.

This indoctrination isn't extreme or obvious. It comes in a socially acceptable form. As such, it is far more difficult to detect. Because it's hard to detect, it's hard to escape.

This type of indoctrination shapes beliefs over time and influences behavior without force. Within this type of organization, compliance gets rewarded. Deviation is quietly discouraged. Most importantly, the shifting culture often goes unrecognized altogether.

Closing Reflection

Early signals don't always mean something deeper is happening, but don't write them off too quickly. When patterns begin to repeat, behaviors begin to shift, and you suddenly have to navigate unspoken rules instead of shared values, pay attention. Because the hardest part isn't what happens later. It's recognizing what is happening as early as possible, when it still feels explainable and temporary and you're still deciding whether what you see is real.

Micro-reflection

What initially drew you to your current or past organization?

At what point—if any—did your experience begin to conflict with your expectations?

What early signs did you notice but explain away or minimize?

How did your need for stability, belonging, or purpose influence your willingness to adapt?

Looking back, what do you now see more clearly that you could not see at the time?

Were you evaluating the system clearly or adapting to it before you fully understood it?

Chapter 2

WHAT MAKES A SYSTEM CULT-LIKE?

What makes a system powerful is not how extreme it appears but how normal it feels. What distinguishes organizational indoctrination is not extremity. It is normalization, and that normalization makes it sustainable.

Not All Difficult Workplaces Are the Same

Not every challenging workplace is structured. Some are disorganized, under-resourced, or led by individuals who lack experience or skill. These environments can be frustrating or even harmful, but they're not necessarily built around control.

I've worked in environments like this too—where challenges were real but visible. In these environments, problems could be openly named, addressed, and improved, even if imperfectly.

That's an important distinction. What separates a difficult workplace from a cult-like system is not dysfunction. It's consistency in multiple areas, including how behavior is shaped and power is maintained.

There is consistency in how people quickly learn what's safe and what's not.

Moving Beyond the Stereotype

When people hear the word cult, they often think of extremes. Isolation, rigid belief systems, and charismatic, unquestioned leaders come to mind. None of these images is wrong, but each is incomplete.

The underlying mechanisms that define cult-like systems aren't limited to extreme environments. They exist in respected places that appear professional and mission-driven.

I've seen these dynamics inside organizations that outwardly looked healthy. Inside their doors, these places do meaningful work and are staffed by capable and well-intentioned people. This doesn't mean they're not cult-like. It just means they're more difficult to recognize, because nothing about them screams, "Cult!"

What Defines a Cult-Like System

At their core, these systems are defined not by appearance but by structure. They rely on a set of reinforcing elements, including:

- Behavioral conditioning through reward and consequence
- Centralization of authority
- Control of information
- Reinforcement of loyalty
- Suppression of dissent

Individually, any one of the above is easily explained away. Together, they combine to create something far more powerful and sinister—a system that teaches control without ever demanding it.

The Core Elements of Organizational Indoctrination

These cultish systems aren't built overnight. They emerge through repetition and reinforcement, consistently rewarding compliance, and quietly discouraging questions.

1. Control of Information

Information is rarely restricted outright. It's simply managed. In such environments, I've seen teams operate with entirely different understandings of a single decision, each believing they had the full picture.

Example: Two teams receive different explanations. Each explanation is partially accurate, and neither is complete. Over time, employees experience the following:

- Limited access to full decision-making context
- Inconsistent communication across organizational levels
- Transparency that varies depending on audience
- Certain conversations that happen in smaller circles
- Certain realities that are softened or not shared at all

This creates dependency. After all, when individuals lack information, they rely more heavily on those who control it. That causes a shift in reliance from practical to structural.

2. Loyalty as Currency

In healthy organizations, trust is built through performance, integrity, and collaboration. In controlled systems, loyalty becomes the primary currency. This loyalty is never defined explicitly. It's inferred through agreement with leadership, alignment with messaging, and absence of visible challenge.

Those who demonstrate loyalty get rewarded. Perks include:

- Access
- Opportunity
- Protection

Those who don't demonstrate unquestioning loyalty get overlooked, questioned, or quietly sidelined. These sidelined professionals may be the most capable within an organization. Despite this, their lack of loyalty results in a lack of advancement.

Over time, that pattern becomes clear. The message is never stated directly, but it is understood: Belonging requires alignment.

3. Suppression of Dissent

Dissent is rarely prohibited within a cult-like environment. Rather, dissent is made too costly to attempt. Employees may be encouraged to share feedback, raise concerns, and engage in open dialogue, but there is no real desire to hear such commentary. The lack of response proves it. To employees who are paying attention, this missing feedback tells the real story.

I've even been in environments where feedback was welcomed in language but punished in practice. Again, this punishment wasn't always overt, but it was very real. The punishment came in subtle shifts in tone, increased scrutiny, and reduced access or opportunity.

Over time, the punished individuals begin to self-regulate, because they learn that silence is safer.

4. Leader-Centric Authority

In these systems, leadership goes beyond influence. It is central to every team member's ability to function. Direction, interpretation, and meaning in these systems may flow from a small group of select few or a single individual.

This concentrated power creates constant dependence on leadership for clarity and reduced tolerance for challenge. Leadership may not demand loyalty outright, but systems form around them that protect their authority, reinforce their perspective, and filter opposing viewpoints.

Eventually, this type of structure causes leadership to expand beyond a source of direction to become a filter for reality. Once this occurs, questioning leadership equates questioning the organization itself.

5. The Reward and Consequence System

The most powerful mechanism isn't what's said in a cult-like organization. Rather, it's what gets reinforced.

People watch and notice who gets promoted, included, and excluded. They see who leaves and under what circumstances. These observations answer the unspoken question: What happens if I do this? Then the system responds, and individuals adjust.

The Subtle Shift in Belief

One of the most overlooked aspects of indoctrination is that it doesn't just influence behavior. It influences belief.

Over time, indoctrinated individuals may begin to:

- Accept explanations they once questioned
- Justify decisions they once challenged
- View dissent as unnecessary or even disruptive

This shift isn't forced. There's no need. It's reinforced every time alignment is rewarded. Since dissonance is uncomfortable, the mind adjusts.

Why It Feels Normal

Perhaps the most concerning aspect of these systems is that from the inside, they often feel normal. Because patterns are consistent, expectations are clear, and consequences are predictable, new employees adapt quickly. Existing employees learn to recalibrate, and the system continues marching on, largely unquestioned. Not because it's invisible, but because it becomes familiar.

A Critical Distinction

It's important to distinguish between structure and control.

Healthy organizations allow disagreement without punishment and share information transparently. They distribute power appropriately and reward performance and integrity.

On the other hand, control-based systems filter information, centralize power, and reward alignment over truth. They make dissent costly. Very costly.

As this makes clear, structure isn't the problem. Control without accountability is.

Recognizing the Pattern

These systems are not defined by a single moment, but rather patterns that repeat across time and context. If you begin to notice consistent reward for alignment, consistent cost for dissent, and consistent control of information, what you're experiencing isn't random. It's structured.

Why This Matters

Seeing and understanding these elements is not just about recognition. It's about positioning. Because only then—once you can identify how the system operates, what it reinforces, and where power is concentrated— can you begin to understand your place within the system.

Once you reach this point, a new question emerges. You no longer ask whether adaptation happens, but how?

Closing Reflection

Cult-like systems do not require extreme beliefs or isolation. They require something far more common—a structure that rewards alignment, manages perception, and quietly discourages challenge. Within that structure, people do what people have always done: they adapt.

The question is not whether adaptation happens. It is how it takes place.

In the chapters that follow, you'll see three clear paths an individual can take inside these systems:

- Assimilate
- Exist
- Resist

When inside one of these systems, you must ask one other important question: Are the patterns you're experiencing isolated or do they reflect a consistent system at work?

Micro-reflection

Which elements of control (information, loyalty, dissent, authority, reinforcement) are most visible in your environment?

Where have you seen information managed rather than openly shared?

How is loyalty defined and how is it rewarded?

What happens when someone challenges a decision or asks difficult questions?

Do leadership structures encourage broad perspectives or reinforce a narrow one?

Chapter 3

THE RECRUITMENT HOOK

People don't commit to systems. They commit to what they believe these systems are. No one joins an organization expecting to be controlled. They join because they believe in something—a mission, a purpose, an opportunity to contribute, grow, and be part of something meaningful.

That is where it all begins.

The Power of Purpose

The most effective systems don't start with control. They start with alignment.

Organizations—especially those in public service, healthcare, nonprofit, and mission-driven sectors—lead with language that resonates deeply. Some of their typical language includes:

- "We're making a difference."
- "This work matters."
- "We serve something bigger than ourselves."

For many professionals, this messaging is appealing on a personal level. It connects to their identity, because they're decent people who want to do good work.

I've been in those spaces, places where the mission genuinely mattered, where the work aligned with purpose, and where you felt called to give your best. That's what makes this stage so powerful. Because when work becomes tied to identity, it becomes more than a job. It becomes something worth committing to fully.

"We're Different Here"

The message is often communicated early—sometimes directly, sometimes subtly. The idea is that this place is different. Leadership may state that "We're not like other organizations" or that "We hold ourselves to a higher standard."

Other times, the message is implied through carefully told stories, curated examples, and how leadership presents the organization.

I've worked for agencies that sold the message exceptionally well. I suspect you have too.

Leadership in these organizations position the company as the exception, that they're different from toxic environments. More evolved, more aligned, more ethical.

Initially, this promise feels true. But that changes. Eventually it becomes clear that the only difference between a healthy and sickly organization isn't the absence of dysfunction but rather the ability to hide it well, at least for a season.

In some cases, the built-in belief that an organization is different becomes part of the problem. That belief actually prevents the system from recognizing what it actually is.

The Illusion of Transparency

During recruitment, organizations highlight what they want you to see.

- Achievements
- Impact
- Opportunity

• Strengths

All of this is expected. But in controlled systems, something more is happening. There, information isn't just curated. It's selectively withheld.

As a result, candidates are rarely told how decisions are actually made or how dissent is truly handled. The interviewing professional won't explain what happens when someone challenges leadership or disclose the informal rules that govern advancement. They smile while they feed one misleading line after another.

I know, because I've sat in on interviews and onboarding sessions during which everything sounded aligned. Clear values, strong leadership, and open communication were promised.

There was just one problem: those statements were incomplete, leaving the new employee to feel a sense of clarity until experience fills in the gaps with real knowledge.

Gaslighting at the Front Door

One of the most overlooked aspects of recruitment is how early gaslighting begins. When it starts early, it's not used as an overt tactic, but as a subtle framing of reality.

The gaslighting statements sound innocent enough, but they have vicious undercurrents.

"We're very collaborative here." But dissent is discouraged.

"We value transparency." But information is tightly controlled.

"We support our staff." But only under certain conditions.

When inconsistencies appear later that can't be ignored, individuals often question themselves. They feel they misunderstood or expected too much. Again, I've had those exact thoughts.

When experience doesn't match clearly laid out expectations, the first instinct is often not to question the system. It's to question yourself. Thus begins the cycle.

Targeting the Right People

These systems tend to attract purpose-driven, highly committed individuals who are willing to go above and beyond and are deeply connected to their work.

These characteristics aren't weaknesses. They're strengths that can be leveraged in environments that blur boundaries, elevate mission above individual well-being, and frame sacrifice as commitment.

In my professional experience, I have watched high-performing, principled individuals enter these systems with the best intentions. Over time, these people slowly adjust to their environment in ways they never could have expected.

The Emotional Contract

Beyond the formal job offer, there is often an unspoken agreement that if you believe in this work, you will give more. More time. More energy. More flexibility.

At first, this extra effort feels voluntary, a reflection of passion and a sign of commitment. When I bought into this false narrative, I gave my all. It didn't feel like deception. It felt like growth and dedication. I didn't recognize what was being normalized was expectation.

Over time, what was once considered above and beyond becomes baseline.

Early Signals Are Often Explained Away

Even during recruitment and onboarding, there are indicators flashing for those with eyes to see. Unfortunately, they're easy to dismiss, especially to optimistic go-getters.

These indicators include:

- Vague answers to direct questions
- Overemphasis on loyalty and "fit"
- Subtle discomfort when probing deeper

• High praise for individuals who “go along”

Individually, these signals seem minor. Together, they form a pattern that is often overlooked when the opportunity feels meaningful, the environment feels welcoming, and the mission feels important. Remember—when something feels important, people are more willing to overlook inconsistency.

Onboarding: Where Normalization Begins

Onboarding in these poisonous environments isn’t just informational. It is cultural conditioning.

This is the avenue in which individuals learn how things are done, what’s expected, and what’s actually valued.

In healthy systems, onboarding encourages curiosity, clarity, and open dialogue.

In controlled systems, onboarding also introduces normalization or unacceptable practices. These introductions come with a few common phrases, such as:

- “It’s just how things work here.”
- “You’ll understand over time.”
- “That’s not something we question.”

These aren’t directives. They’re cues that shape behavior quickly.

Belonging Before Understanding

One of the most powerful forces at this stage is the desire to belong. After all, most new employees are often excited, and they’re eager to prove their value.

They want to fit in, make meaningful contributions, and be seen as capable and aligned with the organization’s stated mission and vision.

As a result, they observe before questioning and adapt before challenging. They’re willing to accept without fully understanding. For them, belonging often comes before awareness.

By the time inconsistencies become clear, adaptation is already in full swing.

The Subtle Shift

At some point, the internal question changes. The employee stops asking "Is this organization the right place for me?" and starts to ask "How do I succeed here?"

This shift is critical. It redirects attention away from evaluating the system and toward adapting to it.

Why This Stage Matters

The recruitment and onboarding phase sets the foundation for everything that follows. It shapes expectations, behavior, perception, and identity. Once those expectations are internalized, they're difficult to unlearn. Because they are not just about what you do, but also where you belong.

A Necessary Distinction

If you've been in a healthy organization, you know that strong recruitment and onboarding are not the problem. This is a time for organizations to inspire commitment, communicate purpose, and set high expectations.

What comes next is where you can start to smell hints of disease.

Healthy systems remain open to challenge, adjust when inconsistencies arise, and value individuals beyond alignment.

Controlled systems do the exact opposite. They reinforce early expectations, dismiss or redirect challenge, and shape individuals to fit the system rather than evolving the system to serve its people.

Closing Reflection

No one enters an organization expecting to be conditioned. They enter because they believe in the mission, leadership, and the possibility of meaningful work. When this belief is met with reinforcement, expectation, and subtle distortion, something more powerful than policy arises. That powerful something becomes the foundation of adaptation.

Micro-reflection

What promises or messages initially drew you into the organization?

Where have your experiences not aligned with what was communicated during recruitment or onboarding?

Have you ever questioned your own perception when something didn't feel right? If so, why?

What language or messaging has been used to normalize or explain inconsistencies?

How much of your commitment is tied to the mission and how much is tied to the reality of the system?

Are you holding onto what the organization said it was or responding to what it consistently shows itself to be?

Chapter 4

CONDITIONING BEGINS

People aren't controlled by force. They're shaped by what's rewarded and tolerated.

No one announces the transition. There is no moment when someone says, "We are now moving from orientation to conditioning." No one passes out a memo or holds a meeting to update employees. No clear line is drawn, but it's there, as clear as day.

By the time most people recognize it, they're already so deep inside the organization that it can be daunting to seek a pathway out.

From Learning to Adapting

At the beginning, employees spend their time learning and absorbing an organization's policies and procedures and their own roles and responsibilities. They try to understand how to do their job and focus on one question: "What is my role?"

Eventually that changes, and the question becomes, "What is expected of me here?"

Those are not the same question, and unfortunately, expectations in controlled systems are rarely written. They are observed and—more importantly—felt.

Why People Are Susceptible to Conditioning

Conditioning works because it aligns with human behavior. People are wired to seek belonging, avoid rejection, and interpret social cues. As a species, we've mastered the art of adapting to our environment. When a power differential enters the scene, all these instincts intensify.

Every organization includes a hierarchy of some sort. In controlled systems, that hierarchy becomes more than the influence that rules thought and action. Because when access, opportunity, and evaluation are tied to a small group, people pay attention to what is said, what isn't said, and what is rewarded.

In Groups and Out Groups

Over time, subtle divisions begin to form. You can recognize who's included and trusted. They're given access everyone wants. The remaining personnel are left on the periphery, observing and navigating carefully to avoid stepping on an eggshell. No one labels these groups, but everyone knows who they are.

This occurs across organizations. Proximity to power changes how individuals are treated, how they are heard, and how much room they are given. Once those dynamics are visible, behavior begins to shift. Because people want more than success. They want to belong.

The First Adjustment

Conditioning doesn't begin with a major decision, but a small one. So small it's often invisible to everyone except the person being conditioned.

An employee considers asking a question and decides not to. They made the choice not because they were told not to, but because the room feels tense, the timing feels off, or the response feels uncertain.

They may soften the question, reframe it, or drop it entirely.

At the moment, it seems minor, but this minor self-redirection is the first moment someone chooses safety over expression. Once that choice is made, it becomes easier to make again.

Normalization Through Observation

Conditioning isn't taught. It's observed. Employees begin to notice who is praised, promoted, and excluded. They see when the person who questions directly becomes labeled or the colleague who challenges decisions becomes less visible. They also see that the one who aligns quickly moves forward.

No one explains these outcomes, but they don't need to. After all, people learn quickly that what happens to others can happen to them as well.

Social Norms Take Hold

As patterns repeat, they become unwritten, social norms. Social norms are powerful because they're enforced collectively.

When these norms begin to have effect, people begin to mirror behavior. They adjust their tone, opt for aligning language, and avoid certain topics because deviation becomes uncomfortable and belonging matters more than most people realize.

Language as Reinforcement

Language, particularly through redirection, is one of the most effective tools of conditioning. It sounds like:

- "That's just how things work here."
- "You'll understand over time."
- "It's bigger than what you're seeing."

These redirections reposition conversation and signal that your perspective is incomplete, the system requires no explanation, and this is not open for debate. This language can be shocking the first time, but individuals stop hearing this language eventually. Then they begin to use it.

The Expansion of Expectations

What begins as voluntary becomes expected. Staying late becomes standard, being constantly available becomes assumed, and taking on more becomes normalized.

When someone doesn't meet expectations, it's noticed. You hear and feel it through tone, feedback, perception, and gestures.

Effort is no longer measured against role. It's measured against culture, and culture is rarely defined clearly.

The Internal Shift

As conditioning deepens, your internal dialogue changes. Instead of wondering if something makes sense, you wonder if it's worth addressing. You stop asking if something is right and start weighing what would happens if you say something.

This is the point at which professional judgment becomes psychological negotiation and clarity is replaced by calculation.

The Role of Ambiguity

Conditioning thrives in ambiguity. When expectations aren't explicit, people interpret, adjust, and self-regulate.

By arriving at those conclusions without explicit coercion, the behavior feels voluntary and not imposed. That's what makes it effective.

The Gradual Acceptance

Over time, what was once uncomfortable becomes normal due to repetition. People incrementally and unconsciously accept inconsistencies, overlook contradictions, and adjust expectations.

The Disappearance of the Line

One of the most defining features of conditioning is the loss of clear boundaries. What is acceptable, expected, and required becomes blurred. Fuzzy.

People then rely less on policy or stated values and more on their observations and experience. Once that happens, the system becomes even harder to challenge. Because at this point, the system is no longer anchored to something visible. It is a force in and of itself.

Why It Works

Conditioning works because it doesn't fight against human nature. It uses it, manipulating the human desire to belong, the instinct to avoid risk, and the tendency to adapt.

People don't change to match the system's demands because they're weak. They change because they recognize change around them and respond in turn.

Closing Reflection

Conditioning does not feel like control. It feels like minor shifts, subtle changes in behavior and perception in response to small decisions. But over time, those shifts accumulate. Then what once felt like a workplace begins to be something else altogether, something operating under a different set of rules that are rarely written but widely understood. By the time those rules are clear, most people are already following them without anyone imploring them to do so.

Micro-reflection

What behaviors seem to carry subtle consequences?

When was the last time you chose silence over expression? Why?

Do you feel clear on expectations at your job or are you interpreting them based on observation?

Where do you see in-groups and out-groups forming, and how does that impact behavior?

Are you acting from clarity or calculation?

Chapter 5

LEADERSHIP AS THE ANCHOR OF CONTROL

CULTURE IS NOT WHAT LEADERSHIP says, but what leadership consistently reinforces.

No system sustains itself without reinforcement, and policies don't enforce culture. Statements don't shape behavior, and intentions don't determine outcomes. People do all of this and more.

Within any organization, no group has more influence over what is reinforced, ignored, or allowed than leadership.

Not Always Intentional

It is important to reiterate that intent does not prevent impact and to understand that systems evolve based on what is reinforced, not what is intended. It's also important to note that all leaders don't set out to create controlled environments. In fact, many do not.

I've worked with and alongside leaders navigating immense pressure—balancing performance demands, public scrutiny, limited resources, and competing priorities. In these moments, decisions are often made quickly by necessity. These decisions are made pragmatically and sometimes reactively.

While these decisions may not be rooted in control, they can still create it. Because repeated responses become patterns that develop into systems.

What Leadership Reinforces Becomes Culture

Despite what HR may claim, culture isn't defined by mission statements. It's defined by behavior.

Specifically, it's built to mirror what leadership rewards, tolerates, ignores, and corrects.

Employees are always watching and answering a critical question: "What actually matters here?" The answer, as you likely know, is rarely found in formal messaging. It's found in outcomes.

The Drift Toward Alignment

In high-pressure environments, alignment feels efficient. It speeds decision-making, reduces conflict, and creates the appearance of cohesion.

For leadership, this can feel necessary, even responsible.

However, such a preference for alignment can quietly shift into expectation. When this happens, leaders may surround themselves with yes-men, individuals who don't challenge decisions. Anytime dissent arises, it's viewed as disruption rather than contribution aimed at improving the organization.

This oft-unintentional shift narrows perspective and further reduces the system's ability to self-correct.

The Role of Middle Leadership

Executive leadership sets direction, but middle leadership sustains the system. These managers, supervisors, and directors interpret expectations, enforce culture, and gate-keep opportunity.

Each day, they're tasked with translating strategy into behavior and leadership tone into team dynamics. Fulfilling these duties is remarkably difficult, as they do so under pressure.

Unlike so many in an organization, middle leaders are accountable in two directions:

- Upward toward upper management, who rewards or penalizes performance
- Downward toward their team, who makes their jobs easier or harder through compliance or rebellion

They do all this with limited authority but significant responsibility. When standing on such a precarious perch, stability becomes the priority. In controlled systems, stability often comes in the form of reinforcing alignment.

Avoiding Disruption

Leadership is often tasked with maintaining order, meeting goals, managing risk, and protecting the organization. Disruption becomes something to manage—not always because it's wrong, but because it's unpredictable.

Dissent introduces uncertainty and potential escalation. In systems already under pressure, safety wins, and leaders often choose containment over exploration. They minimize concerns not because they lack validity, but because addressing them would require disruption. And disruption is costly.

The Narrative of Infallibility

Over time, leadership can take on an elevated position culturally. Decisions are rarely questioned openly, but they're framed as informed and intentional. If anyone speaks against those decisions, the decisions get defended, even when outcomes are unclear.

This creates a quiet but powerful narrative, that leadership knows best. Once that narrative takes hold, nothing good comes of it. Alternative perspectives diminish, critical thinking shrinks, and accountability weakens. Questioning leadership begins to feel like questioning the organization itself, so good employees do what good employees do—they stay quiet.

The Gap Between Perception and Reality

One of the most important and most overlooked dynamics is that leadership and staff often experience the same organization very differently.

Where leaders see progress, strategic alignment, and positive outcomes, staff members experience inconsistency, limited transparency, and uneven application of expectations. Leadership often doesn't recognize the gap, but they reinforce it.

Such reinforcement is especially prevalent in systems where information filters upward and dissent is minimized or eliminated before it can reach top-tier decision-makers. As a result, leadership may genuinely believe the system is functioning effectively, while those within it are adapting in ways that suggest otherwise.

When Leadership Becomes the System

At a certain point, leadership goes beyond guiding the organization and becomes central to how the system operates. Direction, interpretation, and meaning flow through a limited set of individuals established by leadership.

When that happens, flexibility decreases, feedback loops weaken, and change becomes more difficult since altering the system requires challenging the structures that sustain it.

A Necessary Distinction

Strong leadership isn't the issue. In fact, clear direction, accountability, and decision-making authority are essential. The distinction lies in how leadership uses its influence.

Healthy leadership in action encourages challenge without consequence and shares information transparently. These leaders distribute influence appropriately and remain open to correction, because they see the opportunity for growth and improvement.

Control-based leadership doesn't care for either of these positive fruits. So, these leaders prioritize alignment over accuracy, while limiting information access, reinforcing proximity-based influence, and avoiding or suppressing disruption.

Despite how subtle these behaviors are, the impact is anything but subtle.

The Responsibility of Influence

Beyond shaping outcomes, leadership shapes environments, which shape behavior. This shaping structure means that leadership—whether intentionally or not—plays a defining role in the following:

- Whether indoctrination takes hold
- Whether dissent is possible
- Whether individuals feel safe to engage honestly

This isn't about blame. It's about awareness. Without awareness, the system sustains itself.

Closing Reflection

Organizations don't become controlled environments on their own. They become that way through patterns that are reinforced, repeated, and sustained over time.

Leadership sits at the center of those patterns, not always as the cause but always as the anchor. If and when leadership recognizes what is being said and reinforced, this opens the first potential door of opportunity to changing the system.

Because culture shifts don't occur through intention but through leadership willing to see reality and take action.

Micro-reflection

What behaviors does leadership consistently reward in your environment?

What behaviors are tolerated even when they contradict stated values?

Who has access, and how does that shape influence?

How does leadership respond to challenge—with engagement, redirection, or avoidance?

Is alignment prioritized over accuracy?

If nothing changed in how leadership responds today, what would the culture of your current organization look like one year from now?

Chapter 6

THE REWARD AND PUNISHMENT ECONOMY

THE SYSTEM DOES NOT NEED TO EXPLAIN itself. It teaches through consequence.

No one needs to formally explain how an organization works. It explains itself—not through policy or training, but through what happens. As stated previously, these happenings occur consistently, predictably, repeatedly for all to see and learn from.

The Unspoken Equation

Every organization operates with incentives. Some are formal, such as:

- Performance metrics
- Promotion criteria
- Evaluation standards

In controlled systems, the most powerful incentives are unwritten, forming an unspoken order of operations.

Alignment > Access > Opportunity > Reinforced Alignment

Once this cycle begins, it sustains itself when fed by people who can see the pathway to success inside the system.

How People Learn the System

Employees begin by observing who moves forward, who stays in place, and who disappears. As they observe, they quietly wonder what rewarded and disciplined people did differently.

The answer becomes clear through a pattern, as those who advance tend to align with leadership tone and messaging and avoid visible dissent. Those climbing the corporate ladders within these environments have no qualms with reinforcing decisions, even when the purpose and validity are hard to measure. They also keep themselves as close as possible to those in power.

This can be confusing for onlookers, as those who don't advance may be highly capable, strong performers respected by their peers. But because they question too directly, push too consistently, or fail to align visibly, their trajectory shifts. It doesn't lead toward further promotion. It often leads down the hall and out the door.

The Subtlety of Reward

Reward in these systems is rarely formal. It's relational, showing up as inclusion in key conversations, informal access to leadership, early access to important information, and positive framing in decision-making spaces.

These rewards are powerful. They increase visibility, signal trust, and create momentum. Most importantly, such rewards aren't distributed equally. They're distributed solely in alignment with behavior.

Punishment Without Announcement

Punishment in controlled systems is rarely explicit and typically comes with no formal consequences. You won't receive written warnings or clear declarations.

Instead, you'll get left out, receive slower responses to questions, reduced engagement, and subtle shifts in tone.

At first, these changes are difficult to interpret. Like other oddities mentioned in previous chapters, they can be explained away. But once again, they form a pattern. Once the pattern is recognized, it becomes life-giving instruction.

The Power of Exclusion

From the playground to the board room, exclusion is one of the most effective forms of control. It is quiet, plausible, and difficult to prove, but it packs a serious punch.

Exclusion strips an individual of influence, visibility, and opportunity. Covert as it may seem, the excluded individual feels it. So do others.

That shared awareness reinforces the system by saying a silent message: "This is what happens when you step outside the line."

Learning Without Being Told

No one needs oral instructions in these environments. People learn by watching.

The colleague who raised concerns is now less visible. The employee who aligned is now advancing. The team member who stayed quiet remains stable.

These observations answer critical questions:

- What happens if I speak?
- What happens if I stay silent?
- What happens if I align?

Once those answers are clear, behavior adjusts.

The Internal Calculation

Over time, individuals begin to calculate, and professional judgment becomes psychological negotiation. Instead of looking for ways to provide the best work possible, once-idealistic employees begin to act based on their perception of the following:

- Risk vs. reward

- Visibility vs. safety
- Integrity vs. consequence

They also begin asking questions, including:

- Is this worth saying?
- What will this cost me?
- What do I gain by staying aligned?

At this point, behavior stops being driven solely by role or responsibility but by anticipated response.

When Merit Becomes Secondary

In healthy systems, performance drives opportunity. In controlled systems, performance still matters, but it's not enough.

Here, alignment becomes the multiplier.

Two individuals who deliver the same outcomes and perform at the same level have different experiences. The one who aligns more closely advances faster, gains more access, and receives more opportunity, leaving the other in the proverbial dust.

The Reinforcement Loop

Such a system operates through repetition.

Behavior is observed, the system responds, individuals adjust, and the adjusted behavior is rewarded. Rinse and repeat until the behavior becomes normalized.

The Organizational Impact

Over time, these behaviors grow the system that reshapes the organization. This leads to a world of problems, including reduced thought diversity, increased conformity, slower risk identification, and greater error vulnerability.

Why? Because when alignment becomes safer than accuracy, truth takes a back seat.

The Human Cost

For individuals, the impact accumulates over time. Decent

people in these systems may grow frustrated with inequity and feel confused about expectations. Experience this long enough, and they may disengage from work and struggle internally about how to respond.

Some of these will adapt, others will withdraw, and a few will push back. None remains unaffected.

A Necessary Distinction

All systems reward behavior and create consequences. The difference lies in what is reinforced.

Healthy systems reward:

- Accountability
- Constructive challenge
- Integrity
- Performance

Controlled systems reward:

- Alignment
- Proximity to power
- Silence
- Stability

The mechanisms may look similar, but the outcomes are not.

The Turning Point

At some point, individuals who stick around long enough recognize the patterns and incentives and consequences. They then make a choice to align, exist, or resist.

This is when adaptation becomes identity.

Closing Reflection

The reward and punishment economy doesn't need visibility to be effective. It operates through observation, repetition, and response.

Once individuals understand how the system responds, they

respond based on what they learned from the system. And what people learn through consistent reinforcement becomes how they operate.

This is how the system continues without explaining itself.

Micro-reflection

Who is consistently rewarded at you organization and for what behaviors?

What subtle consequences follow when someone challenges the system?

Where do you see exclusion being used and how does it impact behavior?

Are advancement and opportunity tied more to performance or alignment?

What calculations do you find yourself making before speaking or acting?

Are you responding based on what is right or based on what the system has taught you is safe?

Chapter 7

THE INDOCTRINATED (THE LOYALISTS)

Indoctrination is not imposed. It is accepted, one adjustment at a time.

There is a moment—rarely obvious, almost never dramatic—when alignment becomes assimilation. This transformation unfolds gradually through repetition, reinforcement, and subtle shifts in what feels acceptable, expected, and necessary to succeed.

By the time it's visible, it's too late. Behaviors and mindset are already embedded.

At First, It Looks Like Commitment

Previous chapters pointed out that new employees enter with energy, belief in the mission, and a willingness to learn. They come ready to observe, listen, and adapt. After all, this is what every organization expects.

When these employees enter environments where control replaces culture, this adaptation becomes conditioning and eventually identity.

The Path to Assimilation

Consistency, not force, is at work with indoctrination.

Patterns emerge regarding who gets promoted and included or ignored and excluded. The signals get repeated and produce clarity.

Those who align visibly, consistently, and without friction move forward. Those who hesitate do not.

Employees accept the unspoken rule that success is not based on performance. It's based on agreement.

Hip to what's going on, individuals stop asking certain questions. They reframe concerns as misunderstandings, soften their language, and adopt the tone of leadership.

At this stage, most would still describe themselves as professional, adaptable, and aligned, but something more has happened.

Language as a System

Language is one of the most powerful tools of indoctrination, as it communicates and defines reality. In the systems we're studying, language becomes coded. You often hear "That's just how things work here" or "You need to be a team player." Ask certain questions, and you may learn that "Leadership has a broader perspective" and "You don't have all the information."

These phrases aren't inherently harmful. In fact, they can reflect collaboration and trust inside the right environment. Stick them inside a controlled environments, and they serve a different function. They no longer promote explicit clarity. They shut down conversation by redirecting inquiry, minimizing challenge, and reinforcing hierarchy.

Over time, individuals who hear this language begin to use it as a shield to protect themselves and a signal to show alignment. Once language makes this shift, thinking often follows.

Proximity to Power

Indoctrination grows stronger through access. Remember what we've covered before, that those who align closely with leadership gain visibility, influence, opportunity, and proximity.

Combined, these create a powerful psychological effect.

The closer someone is to power, the more likely they are to justify decisions, dismiss criticism, and reinterpret harm. They're never told to do this. It comes naturally when access creates investment and in turn creates loyalty.

I have seen individuals change through proximity. They couldn't help it. Being close to the system changes your vision.

The Erosion of Dissonance

At some point, most individuals encounter something that doesn't sit right. It may be a decision that feels inconsistent, a colleague treated unfairly, or a process that contradicts stated values.

That moment creates dialogue in a healthy system. In a controlled system, it creates dissonance, which must be resolved.

Indoctrinated individuals resolve this internal dissonance in predictable ways. They suspect there's more to the story, because they're convinced leadership makes all decisions with a good reason. "It's unfortunate," the indoctrinated say, "but necessary."

Each time this is spoken, tension decreases—not because the issue is resolved, but because perception has been adjusted. This causes questions to decrease at the same time justification increases and clarity fades. Reality doesn't change in these instances, just perception.

From Participant to Enforcer

The most significant shift is often the least recognized. At some point, indoctrinated individuals begin to reinforce the system. They redirect concerns, discourage dissent, reinforce expectations, and distance from those who question. In other words, they begin to mimic those in authority over them.

This is often done under the guise of protecting the organization or maintaining stability. The individual claims to be supporting leadership.

Whatever the excuse, the effect is the same. The system no longer relies solely on leadership. It's sustained by those within, making the system self-sustaining.

Why They Stay

It's easy to misunderstand indoctrinated individuals, to see them as blindly loyal and unwilling to see reality. But that picture is incomplete. It makes them look complicit.

However, most didn't choose indoctrination consciously. They adapted over time to what the system consistently rewarded.

Remember, many of these people are highly capable, deeply committed individuals who stay because the system has rewarded them. Their identity becomes tied to their role, and leaving would require re-evaluating their beliefs. Most importantly, they no longer experience the system as harmful.

Of course, this doesn't mean the system is innocent. It isn't. Rather, the perception of the person who has succeeded within it has been shaped to align with it.

The Risk of Silence

Along with affecting individuals, indoctrination reshapes the organization. Loyalty replaces accountability, leading to:

- Accelerated ethical drift
- Unaddressed harm
- Weakened feedback loops

These issues often remain unaddressed because those closest to power are least likely to see the system clearly.

A Necessary Distinction

Alignment doesn't always indicate indoctrination. When agreement and dissent are encouraged, performance and integrity are rewarded, and proximity to power is granted to all, alignment is a sign of a healthy system.

The distinction is seen in whether individuals can question leadership without consequence.

Closing Reflection

Indoctrination does not begin with control, but belonging. It grows through reward, stabilizes through language, and it sustains itself through people who come to believe that protecting the system is the same as protecting the mission.

But the mission and the system aren't always the same. Recognizing the difference is where clarity begins.

Micro-reflection

Where have you seen alignment rewarded more than accuracy?

Have you ever justified something that didn't fully sit right? If so, why?

What language do you hear repeated, and do you use it yourself?

How does proximity to leadership shape perception in your environment?

Have you seen individuals shift from questioning to reinforcing? If so, what changed?

Are your current beliefs shaped by clarity or by what the system has consistently rewarded you to believe?

Chapter 8

THE FRINGE SURVIVORS (THE INVISIBLE ONES)

Not everyone adapts by believing. Some adapt by becoming invisible.

Not everyone assimilates or resists. Most people learn how to exist within the system.

These individuals aren't the loudest voices in the room, and they don't defend leadership, file complaints, or push back publicly.

They are simply present and aware, carefully navigating the space in between. They see what's happening. They understand the patterns and make a decision to survive within the broken system.

The Space Between In and Out

Fringe survivors occupy a position that is both central and unseen. Leadership doesn't fully trust them because they're not fully aligned with the system. They perpetually exist in the middle, where they constantly assess risk.

They learn early that visibility carries consequence and notice who gets labeled "difficult," "not a team player," and "not a good fit." They see how quickly perception shifts and understand that opportunity is not neutral. So, they adjust by learning how to move through the system without triggering it.

The Strategy of Staying Small

Survival in these environments isn't passive. It is precise.

Fringe survivors speak less in meetings, avoid strong or definitive positions, decline involvement in visible conflict, and carefully manage trust. They become highly attuned to tone, timing, and audience, careful to stay quiet at the right time and show just enough agreement to thwart detection.

This may look like disengagement, but it's not. It's calculation.

These individuals know something never said out loud: Being right is not the same as being safe.

Awareness Without Agency

Unlike the indoctrinated, fringe survivors don't lose clarity. They continue to see the inconsistencies and patterns, understand what's going on around them. For this, they pay a price.

Awareness without agency is one of the most psychologically taxing positions an employee can occupy. Despite seeing that values don't match behavior and watching patterns of favoritism, exclusion, or quiet retaliation, the individual feels limited in what they can safely do about it.

The Internal Dialogue

This creates a constant internal negotiation. The fringe survivor constantly asks the following questions:

- Am I overthinking this?
- Is this worth saying something about?
- What happens if I speak up?

These individuals have seen what happens when others miscalculate. This knowledge creates a steady psychological strain that's not loud enough to disrupt daily functioning but persistent enough to follow them home.

The Trade-Off

Fringe survivors exchange stability for opportunity, safety for advancement, and silence over risk. They often plateau—not because they lack ability or ambition, but because advancement requires a level of alignment they can't stomach.

They may watch others move ahead who are less experienced or capable but are more aligned. They understand why these promotions happen, even if no one ever says it out loud.

Living in the Gray

There is a unique exhaustion that comes from living in the middle. Fringe survivors are constantly balancing what they believe, say, and do. They may agree publicly and disagree privately or distance themselves from both leadership and resistance.

This creates a form of professional invisibility that simultaneously protects them from being negatively targeted or positively recognized. They exist in a safe space where they're never fully seen.

The Emotional Landscape

Fringe survivors may experience many negative outcomes of their plight, including:

- Chronic disengagement
- Loss of motivation
- Quiet burnout
- Sense of stagnation

The sad part is that they still care for a long time, but caring without agency is unsustainable. So, many eventually begin to detach as a protection mechanism.

They do their work and meet expectations but avoid

unnecessary exposure as a form of self-preservation.

Why They Stay

Why stay in a system you don't fully support? The question is easy to ask, but the answer is rarely simple.

Fringe survivors stay for financial stability. As caring human beings, they've also built meaningful relationships and continue to believe in parts of the mission. Leaving isn't easy for them.

Therefore, they make calculated decisions to stay where they are and preserve as much of their humanity as possible.

I have seen and experienced this space, a space where leaving isn't immediately possible and resisting is dangerous.

In such an environment, the decision process looks like this:

- Stay
- Navigate
- Endure

The Risk of Long-Term Survival

While this path may feel safest, it carries long-term consequences. Skills can stagnate, confidence can erode, and identity can narrow.

Because survival mode changes how people engage and contribute. More importantly, it changes how people see themselves. And the longer someone remains in that state, the harder it becomes to shift out of it. What began as a strategy becomes a pattern, and patterns are difficult to break.

A Misunderstood Position

Leadership may misidentify fringe survivors as disengaged or unmotivated. Resisters may see them as passive or—even worse—complicit in the system.

Both interpretations miss reality.

Fringe survivors aren't unaware or unmotivated. They're

navigating risk in a system with real consequences for miscalculation.

Moments of Shift

On the fringe survivor's journey are moments when the balance changes and a line is crossed. A decision feels too significant to ignore, and the cost of silence begins to outweigh the risk of speaking.

At those moments, some fringe survivors begin to ask questions, document concerns, seek external perspective, or move toward resistance. Others reinforce their survival strategy or begin planning their exit.

The Power of the Middle

Though often overlooked, fringe survivors represent the largest portion of most poisoned systems. These individuals who are stuck in the middle hold something critical: awareness.

If enough individuals in the middle shift toward questioning, accountability, or exit, the system begins to destabilize.

Because the middle is where systems are either sustained or quietly undone.

Closing Reflection

Fringe survivors are not weak or indifferent. They are individuals who have learned through observation and experience that in certain systems, survival requires restraint.

They carry awareness without power, clarity without influence, and presence without protection. While often unseen and unheard, they're always present. When they begin to move, the system begins to change.

Micro-reflection

Where are you choosing safety over visibility, and why?

What patterns do you clearly see but choose not to act on?

How often are you filtering what you say based on anticipated consequences?

Are you maintaining stability or avoiding risk?

What has this environment required you to silence or suppress?

Are you existing in this system, or are you slowly becoming defined by it?

Chapter 9

THE RESISTERS (THE DISRUPTORS)

THERE IS ALWAYS A RISK IN STEPPING forward, but there is a greater risk in standing still while harm continues.

Every system has a threshold, a point where something happens that can no longer be explained away. For some, that moment passes and they adjust, rationalize, and move on.

Resisters reach that threshold and do something quite different.

The Moment It Changes

Resistance rarely begins as defiance. It begins as a moment of recognition.

I have seen this moment happen in real time. And once it happens, it's almost impossible to reverse. Something shifts internally. The question goes from "Can I work within this?" to "Can I live with this?"

For resisters, the answer is no.

They don't accept the company line that something is simply inconvenient, frustrating, or "how things are."

They see the wrong, and silence is suddenly harder to justify.

The Early Signals of Resistance

At first, resistance is measured and quiet. The resister asks clarifying questions, requests rationale or documentation about decisions, and raises concerns through appropriate channels. All this is done in a good-faith attempt to align decisions with stated values.

Healthy organizations encourage such moves. Controlled systems claim to encourage such investigations, but questions are interpreted as challenges. Efforts for clarity are seen as criticism. Concern is translated into disruption.

As a result, the system responds.

When the System Pushes Back

Resisters quickly learn that resistance isn't neutral or welcomed. It is managed with an incremental, strategic response.

The resister is suddenly excluded from key conversations. There's a notable tone shift from leadership, and the resister loses access to information and experiences increased scrutiny of work.

At first, even this gets dismissed as a misunderstanding or coincidence. Then the pattern becomes clear, and it becomes obvious that the system is responding.

The Reputation Shift

One of the most powerful mechanisms used against resisters is reputation, via narrative. They're labeled "Difficult," "Not collaborative," "Negative," and "Not aligned."

These labels spread quietly, shaping opportunities, evaluations, and relationships. The individual hasn't changed, but how they are seen has shifted dramatically.

In many systems, this changed perception becomes reality.

Escalation and Visibility

As resistance continues, so does escalation.

Resisters may begin to document issues more formally, utilize internal reporting channels, engage compliance or HR, and seek external consultation.

At this stage, the issue becomes visible, which introduces risk for the individual and the organization. This visibility challenges narrative. And systems built on control aren't designed to absorb that easily.

The Cost of Speaking

Interestingly, most of these organizations have a spoken narrative that encourages people to speak up. The problem is that when they do, resisters may face the following:

- Emotional and psychological strain
- Isolation
- Loss of advancement
- Subtle or direct retaliation

Even in systems with formal protections, there are informal consequences with real cost. Again, policies may exist, but culture determines reality. Resisters know this.

The Ledge

There is a point in resistance that feels like stepping onto a ledge. The resister is exposed, uncertain, and often alone.

The risk of resisting is real. There are substantial consequences and no guaranteed outcome. Despite this, the resister steps forward. Because the risk of speaking pales to the risk of silence.

Silence allows harm to continue and systems to remain unchecked. This negatively affects staff and those being served. For many resisters, this is the deciding factor, what pushes them over the edge.

External Resistance: Crossing the Line

For some, internal efforts are not enough. Resisters go to HR, and concerns are dismissed. Patterns continue and harm escalates.

So, resistance moves outside of the system. Formal complaints are filed, whistles get blown, and reports are made to regulatory or oversight bodies.

This is a shift from navigating the system to challenging it directly. As such, it comes with real consequences that are professional, personal, and emotional. This shift also introduces something systems cannot fully control: exposure.

The Isolation

One of the most consistent experiences among resisters is isolation. Colleagues step back. Even if they agree with the resistance, they're uncomfortable with the risk they accumulate by association.

Left alone, the resister stands in a narrowing space, no longer fully part of the system but still trapped inside it.

The Internal Conflict

Resistance comes with much internal struggle. Resisters wonder if they're doing the right thing, if it's worth the cost to resist, and if their efforts will yield fruit. Like all others, they weigh integrity vs. stability, accountability vs. career risk, and action vs. uncertainty and come up with no clear winner.

So, they do what they must, making decisions in real time with incomplete information and real consequences.

Why They Continue

Resisters don't continue because it's easy but because inaction becomes more difficult than acting. Driven by their own alignment with personal values and a sense of responsibility for harm done by the system to others, they forge ahead.

Doing nothing, for resisters, stops being an option.

The Impact of Resistance

Resisters introduce disruption, and controlled systems aren't designed to handle that. This disruption comes when resisters expose patterns, challenge assumptions, and create pressure for accountability.

Even when dismissed, their impact remains, causing others to wrestle with lingering doubts.

Not All Resistance Is Visible

Resistance does not always look dramatic. Some resist quietly by documenting, refusing to participate in harm, and supporting others behind the scenes.

As such, resistance is not defined by visibility but refusal to fully comply with a system that feels misaligned.

The Aftermath

Resistance changes people, regardless of outcome. Some leave and rebuild, others continue pushing, and yet more are pushed out.

No one leaves unchanged, because resistance reshapes how individuals view the system and themselves.

A Necessary Role

Resisters are often framed as problems. In reality, they are indicators signaling misalignment, risk, and unaddressed harm. Without them, systems become insulated and unquestioned. Eventually, this causes leadership to disconnect from reality.

Despite what leadership says, resisters don't break systems. They reveal them.

Closing Reflection

Resistance is not comfortable or rewarded in the moment. Though rarely without consequence, it is necessary. Because in systems where silence is safer than truth, one person willing to question, document, and speak can begin the wheels of change.

There's risk in stepping onto that ledge, but there is even greater risk in doing nothing. And sometimes the most significant act is not changing the entire system. The most powerful act is refusing to let the system continue operating unseen.

Micro-reflection

Where have you reached a point that no longer feels explainable or acceptable?

What risks are you weighing, and what are you protecting?

What would happen if you spoke up?

What is happening because you have stayed quiet?

Who around you is impacted if nothing changes?

Is the risk of stepping forward greater than the cost of allowing harm to continue?

Chapter 10

THE PSYCHOLOGICAL IMPACT

THE MOST SIGNIFICANT HARM IS NOT always what happens to you but what you begin to believe about yourself.

Not all harm is visible. There are no incident reports or formal documentation for the harm of dwelling in a system of indoctrination. But the damage accumulates quietly and consistently, often going unnoticed.

The Slow Erosion

The psychological impact of controlled systems is rarely immediate. It begins with small shifts—hesitation before speaking, second-guessing, or risk management in ordinary interactions.

These small steps compound into a pattern of slow erosion.

From Clarity to Confusion

One of the earliest impacts is cognitive. Individuals who once trusted their judgment begin to question it. They wonder if they're overreacting, fear they don't have the full picture.

This is not a lack of competence. It is the result of sustained exposure to inconsistency.

When words don't match actions, values don't align with

decisions, and outcomes contradict expectations, the brain attempts to reconcile the gap. When reconciliation is impossible, the brain adjusts, while the system continues forward, unbothered.

Chronic Hypervigilance

Over time, awareness becomes heightened as individuals begin to monitor how they speak, the language they use, and others' reactions to what they say. They scan the air for signs of problems, constantly asking:

- Is this safe to say?
- Who is in the room?
- How will this be interpreted?

This is hypervigilance, an exhausting survival skill that keeps the nervous system in a constant state of alert without resolution.

Moral Injury

This aligns with what is clinically called moral injury: a sustained violation of one's ethical framework in the context of role expectations.

Perhaps the most significant and least discussed impact, then, is not stress. It is moral disruption.

Individuals may participate in decisions they don't fully support. When they feel they should speak up, they remain silent. They align verbally and externally while disagreeing internally.

This creates a fracture between what the individual believes is right and what they feel required to do. This dissonance reaches the very level of personal identity, and it doesn't resolve through rest alone.

The Shift in Identity

Work is often part of who employees are, especially in helping professions, public service, and mission-driven organizations.

When individuals adapt to controlled systems, their identity begins to shift.

They may change how they talk, hesitate more often, and lose confidence. They may become more cautious and less expressive. Eventually, they feel they don't even know themselves.

Emotional Numbing and Detachment

For many, the only sustainable response to life in a controlled system is detachment. They continue to meet expectations while avoiding deeper engagement. Caring without agency becomes overwhelming, so they reduce connection and investment.

This presents as disengagement, reduced motivation, and emotional distance and is frequently labeled as burnout. However, this is more specific than burnout. It is adaptive withdrawal, a response to an environment that does not allow full engagement safely.

The Weight of Silence

Silence carries weight. Each time an individual chooses not to speak out of self-preservation, a new pattern emerges. Silence becomes habitual and expected. Yet it still creates internal tension since the individual knows what they are not saying.

Burnout Redefined

Burnout is often described as emotional exhaustion caused by overwork and long hours. In these systems, burnout has a different profile.

It centers around a lack of control, voice, and alignment. These individuals aren't just tired. They're disconnected, disillusioned, and drained in ways that rest can't resolve.

Because the issue is not workload or lack of vacation time. It is environment.

Learned Helplessness

When individuals repeatedly speak up and raise concerns without response, they adjust their expectations. They stop trying. After all, experience has taught them that nothing changes, despite their greatest efforts.

This is learned helplessness, one of the most dangerous outcomes. It's dangerous because it stabilizes the system without requiring enforcement.

The Fragmentation of Trust

Trust erodes in layers and typically moves in a predictable order. First, you lose trust in leadership, then the organization. Trust in colleagues dissolves soon afterward, which can ultimately lead to loss of trust in self.

Individuals begin to question their perception, reactions, and judgment, creating an internal fragmentation that's difficult to repair.

Different Paths, Different Impacts

The psychological impact of this fragmentation varies depending on how individuals adapt.

Assimilated (indoctrinated) may adapt in the following ways:

- Reduced dissonance
- Strong alignment with system narrative
- Limited awareness of harm

Fringe survivors may experience:

- Chronic internal tension
- Emotional fatigue
- Awareness without agency

Resisters, on the other hand, may notice the following:

- Acute stress
- Isolation
- High emotional and professional risk

The important thing to notice is that each path carries a cost.

Why This Goes Unrecognized

These impacts rarely get addressed because they are difficult to measure. While organizations track productivity, performance, and retention, they're ill-equipped to track internal conflict, moral strain, and psychological adaptation.

Even if these less tangible benchmarks could be measured, controlled systems would overlook them.

The Cumulative Effect

Repeated hesitation, adjustment, silence, and compromise do significant work. Yes, they shape behavior, but they also reshape perception, emotion, identity, and self-concept.

Closing Reflection

The most significant impact of controlled systems is not what they demand but what they change. Along with influencing behavior, these systems reshape how people think and feel and see themselves.

This reshaping is often slow enough that it goes unnoticed. Until one day it can't be ignored any longer, when employees ask, "How much of this is still me, and how much of it is a creation of the system?"

Micro-reflection

Where have you started to question your own judgment and why?

What behaviors have you changed to feel safer in your environment?

Are you experiencing fatigue or disconnection?

What are you no longer saying that you once would have?

Do you feel aligned with your values or adjusted around them?

Who were you before this environment, and who have you had to become within it?

Chapter 11

SYSTEMIC CONSEQUENCES — WHEN THE SYSTEM BECOMES THE RISK

When a system cannot question itself, it becomes the risk it was designed to manage.

The impact of organizational indoctrination extends beyond the workforce, affecting decision-making, service delivery, and outcomes that affect real people—staff, communities, and beyond.

When internal systems prioritize alignment over accuracy, loyalty over accountability, and stability over transparency, the organization does not just shift culturally. It shifts operationally. Eventually, it shifts functionally.

From Internal Pattern to External Outcome

What happens inside an organization does not stay contained. It shows up everywhere you look. In missed warning signs, delayed decisions, and preventable failures.

What causes such widespread chaos? The system's conditioning. It's built and conditioned to respond in predictable ways, which aren't always aligned with reality.

I have seen this across systems. What looks like a sudden failure externally was often visible internally long before.

Case Patterns from Real Systems

The following cases are composites drawn from real-world patterns observed across organizations and systems. These cases are not isolated, and they are repeatable.

Case 1: The Unquestioned Decision

A mid-level leader raises concern about a new directive. The concern appears inconsistent with prior policy, risky in its application, and lacking clear rationale. So, the concern is raised in a professional manner.

The controlled response is cold and calculated. "This has already been decided. Besides, there are factors you're not aware of."

The leader hesitates a moment, then proceeds. No one else raises the concern, and the directive is implemented.

Within months, the following occurs:

- Complaints emerge
- Service quality declines
- Staff confusion increases

But by then, it's too late. The decision is gospel. Reversing it is politically difficult and operationally disruptive. Since the system hates disruption, the system adapts and absorbs the problem as a new way of life.

System Insight

The failure was not the decision alone. It was the absence of effective challenge. A system that cannot tolerate questioning cannot correct itself.

CASE 2: THE DISAPPEARING DATA

A team identifies concerning trends, including:

- Increased incident reports
- Rising staff turnover
- Slower response times

The data gets shared upward and acknowledged, but not centered. Instead, reporting shifts toward positive indicators, selective metrics, and framing that minimizes concern.

While ignored, the data still exists. It just doesn't lead the narrative.

Externally, the organization appears stable. Internally, strain increases, while morale declines and risk builds. Once the issue eventually surfaces, it feels sudden and unexpected. But it was visible all along.

System Insight

When information gets managed instead of confronted, reality doesn't change. Only perception does.

CASE 3: THE HIGH PERFORMER WHO LEFT

A highly capable employee with strong outcomes who is respected by peers and consistently reliable begins raising concerns. These concerns center on inefficiencies and inconsistencies and the impact of both on those being served.

Leadership accepts the feedback and gives a subtle response. They begin offering more critical feedback, narrowing opportunities, and reducing the individual's inclusion.

The employee adjusts, disengages, and then leaves.

As a result, the organization takes a hit, because the lost employee takes the following:

- Expertise
- Institutional knowledge

- Internal credibility

Others observe and adjust their own expectations and behaviors.

System Insight

Retention is not just about keeping people. It's about tolerating certain behaviors.

Case 4: The Escalation That Could Have Been Prevented

Concerns are raised, documented, reported, and escalated internally multiple times. The response, however, is limited. There is acknowledgment without action and redirection without resolution.

Over time, the issue escalates externally. Now the organization faces potential negative consequences, including:

- External investigation
- Legal exposure
- Reputational damage

What could have been addressed early, quietly, and effectively becomes a costly public relations nightmare.

System Insight

When systems suppress internal correction, they increase the likelihood of external intervention.

Patterns Across Systems

Across these cases, the pattern is consistent.

1. **Early signals are present.** Concerns are raised, data presented, and patterns exhibited.
2. **Response is constrained.** The concern is minimized and contained, and the person who presented the concern is redirected.

3. **Behavior adjusts.** Fewer people speak, and this risk tolerance allows for the continued filtering of information.
4. **Impact escalates.** Outcomes decline, issues rise to the surface, and intervention becomes necessary.

This is a systemic pattern that healthy companies don't experience.

The Cost of Alignment Over Accuracy

When systems prioritize alignment, a few things happen.

- Decisions go unchallenged
- Errors go uncorrected
- Risk goes unmanaged

This is a problem, because accuracy requires dissent, debate, and disruption. In controlled systems, such things are fought against. When they force their way in, they come at a cost.

The Illusion of Stability

From the outside, these organizations often appear stable. Metrics look acceptable, messaging seems consistent, and leadership appears aligned.

A closer look may show a system that is compensating, absorbing strain, and adjusting around dysfunction.

Put simply, stability is not always a sign of health. It can be a sign of suppression.

Impact Beyond the Organization

For organizations that serve others, the consequences extend beyond internal culture. They affect quality of care, individual safety, decision integrity, and public trust.

When internal systems distort reality, external outcomes follow. The people most affected are often the least visible in the decision-making process.

Why Systems Fail to Self-Correct

In theory, organizations should correct themselves. But controlled systems struggle to do so due to filtered feedback, reduced dissent, and narrow leadership perspectives.

Without accurate input, correction becomes unlikely. Don't misunderstand. The system can change, but it usually cannot see clearly enough to know that it should.

The Accumulation of Risk

Risk in these systems accumulates slowly, as decisions and behaviors give the system what it demands and misses opportunities for correction.

The risk builds quietly and slowly until it becomes excessively complex and nearly impossible to reverse.

A Critical Distinction

Organizational failure isn't always systemic. When structure leads to failure, it's often preceded by the following:

- Managed information
- Reinforced alignment
- Suppressed dissent

Closing Reflection

Organizations fail because of patterns that limit visibility, reduce accountability, and prioritize stability over truth. Those patterns solidify internally long before the impact is visible externally.

Therefore, the most important question is not "What went wrong?" but "What was happening long before anyone was willing to say it out loud?"

Micro-reflection

What early warning signs are visible in your environment right now?

Where is information being minimized, filtered, or reframed?

What concerns have been raised but not acted on?

Who has left, and what did others learn from it?

What risks are currently being absorbed rather than addressed?

If nothing changes, what will this system look like in one year, and who will be affected by it?

Chapter 12

WHY GOOD PEOPLE STAY

People don't stay in a job because they're blind to the system. They stay because leaving is rarely simple.

From the outside, the question seems straightforward. If the system is harmful, the patterns are clear, and the impact is real, why stay?

It is one of the most commonly asked questions posed to those within a harmful system. The problem is that staying is rarely about not seeing. People stay because of what happens after they leave.

This Is Not a Knowledge Problem

Most people who remain in these systems are not unaware. They see the inconsistencies and recognize the patterns. They also understand the risks of leaving.

They may not have language for what they see and feel, but they feel something is off. Over time, that feeling becomes knowledge. Therefore, the decision to stay is not rooted in ignorance but complexity.

The Reality of Stability

For many, the decision is not between staying and leaving. It's between stability and uncertainty.

After all, people have families and financial responsibilities. Leaving, therefore, isn't just a professional decision. It is a life decision, and timing matters.

As with other events in a controlling system, I have seen and experienced this reality. The system is clear, but the exit is not. So, people stay—not because the system works, but because leaving may not.

The Weight of Investment

Over time, people build more than a job. They build careers and reputations and identities, all while cultivating real relationships that matter. This takes years, sometimes decades.

As a result, leaving is not just a transition. It's a disruption that forces a person to let go of what has been built. Leaving means walking away from connections and toward uncertainty.

The deeper the investment, the more complex the decision becomes. These invested individuals aren't trapped. They just recognize the very real cost of leaving.

Belief in the Mission

Even when people struggle with leadership, culture, and internal dynamics, they may stick around because they still believe in the purpose. They believe their work is meaningful and has a positive effect on those being served.

This creates a powerful tension, which can make leaving feel like abandoning something meaningful, even when staying comes at a cost.

The Pull of Hope

There is often a quiet belief that things might improve,

leadership will shift, systems will evolve, and concerns will be addressed.

Such hope is not naïve. Time and again, organizations do change and people do grow. But not always. When the growth and change don't occur, false hope can extend timelines, keeping people in place longer than intended. Waiting, watching, and believing the system will become what it promised to be.

How People Arrive Here

Very few people make a single, conscious decision to stay in a harmful system. They arrive there gradually through small adjustments, minor compromises, and incremental shifts.

Along the journey, every step feels measured and reasonable, temporary and necessary. As those steps accumulate, what once felt like a short-term situation that could be changed becomes a sustained reality.

The Normalization of Discomfort

One of the most powerful forces in staying is normalization. Concern, misalignment, and unacceptable practices transform into expected, manageable, and routine.

All this through repetition, which breeds familiarity.

The Comparison Trap

People rarely evaluate their situation in isolation. They compare it to other environments and figure it could be worse, because it is worse at some places. This reframing makes staying a rational choice.

To reach this choice, the system can't be measured against what's right but against what's worse. That shifts the threshold of what someone is willing to tolerate.

Fear of the Unknown

Leaving introduces uncertainty. Questions emerge, such as:

- Will the next place be better or the same?
- Will I regret leaving?
- What if I lose more than I gain?

For many, sticking with what is known feels safer than venturing into the unknown. Because uncertainty is not just uncomfortable. It's unpredictable.

Identity and Role

As previously stated, work is not just what people do, but who they become—particularly for those in leadership roles, helping professions, and mission-driven environments.

People in these environments see themselves as helpers, experts, and leaders. The thought of leaving due to nonalignment brings up deep questions. These mission-minded people realize that leaving a job redefines their identity.

And that is not a simple transition.

The Quiet Loss of Agency

Over time, individuals in controlled systems notice a reduction in perceived agency shaped by experience and expectation. After concerns go unaddressed and efforts produce little change in the system, action becomes less likely.

This giving up of sorts isn't due to a lack of caring. It's because the individual no longer believes their actions matter.

Different Paths, Different Reasons

The reasons for staying differ across the three paths.

Assimilated (Indoctrinated)

- Align their identity with the system
- Do not perceive the system as harmful
- Feel natural staying

Fringe Survivors

- Manage risk

- Prioritize stability
- Wait for the right moment to act

Resisters

- Attempt to create change
- Navigate consequences
- Prepare to leave

Each path represents a different relationship to the system. All involve a form of staying.

The Absence of a Clear Exit

There is rarely a clear signal that says "Now is the time to get out of Dodge." Instead, there are moments of discomfort, clarity, and questioning.

Turning those moments into action requires timing, resources, and opportunity. Getting these three elements to align perfectly rarely happens.

Reframing the Question

If you see someone inside a controlling system, don't ask "Why do they stay?" Rather, ask "What conditions make leaving difficult?"

When those conditions are understood, you understand that staying becomes less about choice and more about context.

The Quiet Calculation

For most, staying is not passive but calculated. Those staying in place at any given moment have an ongoing internal conversation. They're constantly asking the following:

- What do I gain by staying?
- What do I risk by leaving?
- What can I tolerate?
- What can I not tolerate?

This calculation shifts over time as awareness increases,

circumstances change, and thresholds are defined and overstepped. Until one day, for some, the balance eventually tips.

Closing Reflection

Good people do not stay because they're unaware. They stay because the system is complex, the cost of leaving is real, and such a big decision has layers. At least for a time, staying feels like the most viable option.

Until it doesn't.

When that moment comes, the question becomes "What am I willing to do next?"

Micro-reflection

What are the real reasons you're staying in your current job—not the surface reasons, but the deeper ones?

What are you gaining by staying, and what is staying costing you?

Where has discomfort become normalized in your environment?

What fears are influencing your decision to remain?

If nothing changes, how long are you willing to continue in this space?

Are you staying because it is right for you or because it feels like the safest option right now?

Chapter 13

RECOGNIZING THE SIGNS EARLY

The most dangerous systems don't demand your compliance outright. They teach you to explain everything away.

Most people don't recognize a controlled system at the beginning. The signs are there, but they're subtle and dispersed.

By the time the pattern shows itself, people have usually already adapted to it. They've adjusted behavior, reframed inconsistencies, and learned what is safe to say and do and what's dangerous.

This chapter exists to interrupt that process, to give helpful language, identify patterns earlier, and provide practical ways to assess what's happening in real time.

The Distinction: Normal Friction vs. Systemic Control

Every organization has challenges—miscommunication, leadership gaps, and resource constraints. These don't indicate control. They're an expected part of complexity.

Controlling systems can be detected by looking for pattern and response. When determining if you're inside a controlling system, ask the following questions:

- Are issues addressed or absorbed?
- Are concerns explored or redirected?
- Does feedback lead to change or consequence?

Healthy systems adjust issues, explore new ways of thinking, and change to better align with mission. Controlled systems do the exact opposite.

Section I: Early Warning Signs

Before the system is fully visible, nothing is definitive, but something feels off.

1. Inconsistent Transparency

You may notice information getting shared unevenly across teams. Decisions may get explained differently depending on the audience. You may frequently hear that "There's context you're not aware of."

This signals that information is not being shared. It's being managed.

2. Overemphasis on "Culture Fit"

Common phrases you may hear include "We're very particular about who fits here" or "Not everyone thrives in this environment."

These are true statements. However, no one clearly defines what "fit" or "thrives" actually mean.

These statements signal that alignment is prioritized over diversity of thought, and undefined standards allow flexibility in how people are included or excluded.

3. Subtle Discouragement of Questions

Questions are technically allowed, but responses are vague and the tone shifts when certain topics are raised. Follow-up is limited or avoided.

This signals that dissent is neither prohibited nor safe.

4. High Praise for Loyalty, Low Tolerance for Challenge

Aligned individuals are elevated, while questioners get labeled in meaningful social ways.

This signals that loyalty is currency, and currency determines movement.

5. Early Normalization Language

Commonly used phrases include:

- "That's just how things work here."
- "You'll understand over time."
- "It's bigger than what you're seeing."

Listening closely makes it clear that behavior is being shaped without explanation and lots of expectation.

Section II: Mid-Stage Red Flags

Once the system is formed and functioning, patterns are no longer subtle. They're consistent.

1. Uneven Consequences

You may notice similar behaviors produce different outcomes depending on the individual, and accountability is inconsistent.

This screams that rules aren't the governing structure. Relationships are.

2. Reputation-Based Decision-Making

You hear about difficult, unaligned people, but these abnormalities are never documented, and the problems are never made clear.

When this happens, the signals indicate that narrative is replacing evidence, and perception is driving outcomes.

3. Exclusion Without Explanation

You observe or experience being left out of meetings, losing access to information, and reduced involvement without reason.

This signals punishment without being named.

4. Data That Doesn't Match Reality

Positive reports don't reflect lived experience, metrics get emphasized selectively, and concerns are minimized in reporting.

When you see this, know that perception is being managed and reality is being reframed.

5. Increased Self-Censorship

You may hesitate before speaking, avoid certain topics, and be particularly careful with your wording.

Anytime this occurs, the system is no longer external. It is shaping behavior internally.

Section III: Advanced Indicators

Once the system is fully operational and self-sustaining, the system no longer needs reinforcement. It runs itself.

1. Silence Becomes the Norm

In this final stage, fewer people raise concerns, meetings lack meaningful discussion, and decisions move forward without challenge.

Pay attention, because this signals that psychological safety has left the building, even if it's still boasted about by leadership.

2. Patterned Turnover

Employees consistently leave, particularly those who question or challenge.

This is a clear signal that the system is filtering out resistance to preserve itself.

3. Leadership Isolation

Leadership receives filtered information with limited or softened feedback that has a clear disconnect from staff experience.

Such isolation occurs when the system is protecting leadership from reality.

4. External Issues Appear "Sudden"

Complaints, investigations, and public concerns become rampant over the same issues you've seen on the inside for weeks, months, or years.

This indicates that the internal correction mechanisms have failed and collapse is coming soon.

Section IV: Practical Tools for Real-Time Assessment

These tools are designed for use while inside the system. Use them wisely and well.

Tool 1: The Pattern Test

Ask yourself the following:

- Is this a one-time issue or a repeated pattern?
- Does the same situation produce the same outcome over and over?

If the answer to both is yes, you are seeing a system, not an isolated event.

Tool 2: The Response Test

Observe what happens when someone raises a concern.

Track tone, outcome, and follow-up. Keep in mind that the response tells you more than the issue itself.

Tool 3: The Alignment Vs. Accuracy Test

Ask whether decisions get evaluated based on correctness or agreement.

If agreement is prioritized, alignment is driving the system.

Tool 4: The Risk Calculation Check

Notice your internal dialogue and jot down anytime you ask yourself these questions:

- "Is this worth saying?"
- "What will this cost me?"

When thinking shifts to risk management, you're being conditioned.

Tool 5: The Exit Pattern Review

Look at who has left and ask:

- What do they have in common?
- What behaviors did they exhibit?

Departure patterns often reveal what the system cannot tolerate.

Section V: Red Flag Summary (Quick Reference)

Note the presence of the following:

- Data not reflecting lived experience
- Dissent leading to consequence
- Information being controlled or distributed unevenly
- Loyalty being rewarded more than performance
- Reputation replacing documentation
- Silence increasing over time

If you notice these consistently, you are likely operating within a structured control system.

Section VI: What to Do When You See It

Recognition is the first step, but awareness without response can lead to further adaptation.

Thankfully, you have options.

Option 1: Observe Strategically

- Document patterns
- Maintain clarity
- Track responses

Option 2: Test the System Carefully

- Assess tolerance for dissent
- Evaluate responses
- Raise low-risk questions

Option 3: Strengthen External Perspective

- Avoid isolation in interpretation
- Seek input outside the system
- Validate what you are seeing

Option 4: Protect Your Position

- Be intentional about visibility
- Maintain boundaries where possible
- Manage risk without losing awareness

Option 5: Begin Decision Planning

At some point, recognition leads to choice. You may stay, exist, resist, or exit.

Whichever you choose, the goal is not immediate action but informed decision-making.

Closing Reflection

The most dangerous systems are those that feel normal, where odd signs are present but explainable, patterns are visible but rationalized, and the system's impact is real but gradual.

Recognizing the system early does not make your choice easier. It does, however, make it clearer, and clarity changes everything. Because once you see the system, adaptation is no longer automatic. It becomes a choice.

Micro-reflection

What patterns are repeating that you have explained away?

Where does the system respond differently based on who is involved?

What are you noticing but not naming?

When you raise concerns, what happens next?

Are you adapting because it makes sense or because it feels necessary?

Are you seeing this system clearly, or are you still explaining it in a way that allows you to stay comfortable within it?

Chapter 14

REBUILDING THE SYSTEM

Systems don't change because they are asked to. They change when the sustaining patterns are disrupted.

Recognizing a system is one thing. Changing it is another. Because once patterns of control are established—once behavior, perception, and incentives are aligned—the system doesn't work to correct itself. It does everything necessary to sustain itself.

In the process of self-sustaining, the system will use people, structure, and reinforcement.

As a result, fixing the system requires more than awareness. It requires intervention.

The Reality of System Change

Most organizations believe they can self-correct, and they can—in theory. In practice, controlled systems struggle to change because the system that needs to change is the same system responsible for initiating that change.

Within that system, feedback is filtered, dissent minimized, and leadership perspective narrowed. Incentives reinforce the current state, creating a tricky paradox that prevents meaningful correction unless something interrupts it.

Why Culture Alone Is Not Enough

Organizations often respond to dysfunction with new value statements and culture initiatives. Emails and meetings include messaging about transparency and accountability.

But remember, culture is not what is written. It's what is reinforced. Without structural change, culture messaging becomes aspirational, inconsistent, and ineffective. How can change happen when the underlying system remains untouched?

Real correction requires structural intervention.

Part I: Fixing the System (Leadership & Organizational Level)

Rebuilding a system is not about intention. It is about design.

1. Make Transparency Operational

Transparency cannot be a value. It must be baked into an organization's infrastructure. This requires the following:

- Access to data that reflects reality, without positive framing
- Clear documentation of decision-making processes
- Consistent communication across levels

When transparency is optional, it becomes selective. And selective transparency is not transparency at all.

2. Protect Dissent as a Function, Not a Risk

If speaking up carries risk, people go quiet. Organizations must build mechanisms to make dissent safe, expected, and actionable.

This includes and allows the following:

- Anonymous reporting that gets reviewed and given serious consideration
- Required follow-up and documented response processes
- Structured forums for challenge and not just feedback

The standard must be that dissent leads to engagement and not consequence.

3. Separate Loyalty from Performance

One of the most critical structural failures confuses alignment with effectiveness. Rebuilding requires objective performance metrics, multi-source evaluations, and a clear distinction between behavior and agreement.

Additionally, you must eliminate language that masks bias. This includes phrases such as:

- "Not a good fit"
- "Not aligned"

If something can't be measured, it should not determine outcome.

4. Rebalance Power and Access

Controlled systems concentrate power. Healthy systems distribute it. If you want to build a healthy system, you must do the following:

- Broaden participation in decision-making
- Reduce dependency on proximity to leadership
- Rotate visibility and opportunity

When access determines influence, influence becomes controlled.

5. Build Real Accountability for Leadership

Leadership cannot be the sole evaluator of leadership. There must be independent oversight, external review mechanisms, and measurable accountability tied to behavior (not just outcomes).

True accountability includes:

- Response to dissent
- Retention patterns
- Unfiltered staff feedback

Since leadership shapes the system, those in leadership must be accountable to it.

6. Align Incentives with Integrity

Every system reflects what it rewards. When organizations reward speed over accuracy, alignment over challenge, and outcomes over ethics, those behaviors define the system.

Rebuilding requires intentional reinforcement of positive attributes, including:

- Accountability
- Constructive challenge
- Ethical decision-making
- Transparency

Incentives are never neutral and always directional and educational.

7. Build Feedback Loops That Cannot Be Filtered

Filtered feedback delays correction. To avoid this and build a healthy system, organizations must ensure the following:

- Data reflects actual conditions and not curated narratives
- Direct staff input reaches decision-makers
- Regular review cycles include dissenting perspectives

Systems can't fix what they don't see. Unfiltered feedback ensures problems are put front and center.

What Real Change Looks Like

A system moving toward correction doesn't feel perfect, but it does feel different.

Inside such a system, you'll see increased engagement with difficult questions. Leaders will display greater consistency between language and action and more balanced distribution of opportunity. There is also a reduced reliance on informal reputation.

These healthy patterns are how change becomes visible and lasting.

Part II: What Employees Can Do Inside the System

Not everyone has the authority to redesign a system, but everyone has agency in how they engage with it.

1. Maintain Clarity

Clarity reduces self-doubt, and self-doubt is one of the system's most powerful tools. Gain clarity by doing the following:

- Name what you see
- Identify patterns
- Separate perception from conditioning

2. Don't Just Remember, Document

Memory fades. Patterns do not. Documentation turns experience into evidence, so keep track of the following:

- Decisions
- Outcomes
- Responses

Hold onto this data for long-term clarity.

3. Test the System Strategically

Before escalating, assess the situation. Start small and observe carefully, asking questions such as:

- How does the system respond to low-risk questions?
- Is there space for engagement?

The answers will tell you everything you need to know.

4. Build External Perspective

Controlled systems narrow perception. To fight this, you must expand it intentionally. Do this with the following steps:

- Compare experiences with others
- Seek input from outside the organization
- Validate what you experience

External perspective restores reality.

5. Protect Your Position

Don't act impulsively on what you see. Rather, be intentional about:

- What you say
- When you say it
- Who you say it to

6. Choose Your Path Consciously

You're already on one of three paths:

- Assimilate
- Exist
- Resist

The goal is not to force a path, but to choose it with clarity.

7. Define Your Threshold

Every person has a limit, and the system will test yours. If you do not define your limits, the system will do that for you.

Before the system has a chance, ask yourself the following:

- What am I willing to tolerate?
- What will I absolutely not tolerate?

Your answers provide boundary-establishing clarity.

8. Plan, Don't React

If change becomes necessary, do the following:

- Consider and build your options
- Prepare for a transition
- Strengthen your network

Leaving is most effective when it's intentional and not reactive.

Part III: When Change Is Not Possible

Not all systems will change. Some are too entrenched, too reinforced, too resistant to disruption.

In these cases, give up on fixing the system and determine your relationship to it.

The Hard Truth About Reform

Reforming a controlled system is uncomfortable. It requires disruption. You'll lose any existing advantage you have and must be willing to challenge established patterns. Hence why reform is often resisted.

Even when the need is clear, such change can be difficult, as it affects real people who reap real benefit from the current structure.

Closing Reflection

Systems don't change because they're asked to change. They change because something—or someone—interrupts them.

The interruption can come from leadership, structure, external pressure, or individuals who refuse to fully adapt. Without this interruption, the system continues unchallenged.

The real question isn't whether the system can change but who is willing to disrupt it and what they're willing to risk to be the source of disruption.

Micro-reflection

What structures in your organization reinforce the current system?

Where is transparency missing or selectively applied?

How does your organization respond to dissent in practice and not in policy?

What incentives are shaping behavior right now?

Is change being discussed or structurally implemented?

If nothing structurally changes, what will this system continue to produce, and are you willing to be part of that outcome?

Chapter 15

EXIT, REFORM, OR FIGHT

No path is without cost. What cost you are willing to pay?

By this point, you know what's happening around you. You see the patterns and understand the system. What do you do about it?

Once you ponder this question, the whole thing becomes personal, a lived decision with real-life consequences.

The Weight of Decision

Every person has a moment when awareness becomes responsibility. At this point, observing is no longer enough. Clarity demands choice.

Unfortunately, that choice is rarely clean. There is no option that preserves all you long for: stability, integrity, opportunity, and safety.

Every path comes with benefits, and every decision requires something in return. What are you willing to let go of to walk your path of choice?

Part I: The Three Decision Paths

Everyone inside a controlled system eventually moves toward one of three paths.

1. Stay and Assimilate

This path involves full alignment and full participation in the system as it exists.

This looks like adopting its norms, reinforcing its expectations, and operating within its structure. Perks include:

- Access
- Opportunity
- Reduced internal conflict over time
- Stability

Despite the perks, there is a cost. With this approach, you'll experience the following:

- Gradual loss of independent perspective
- Identity becoming intertwined with the system
- Reframing of behaviors that once felt misaligned

This should not be considered failure. It is adaptation and survival, but it is not neutral.

2. Stay and Navigate (Exist or Selective Resistance)

This path reflects awareness with restraint. You see the system clearly, manage your visibility, and choose carefully when and how to engage.

You may be a fringe survivor here or a strategic resistor. On the plus side, you experience the following:

- Continued employment
- Limited but controlled engagement
- Stability (even though wrought with tension)

The cost of camping out in this area includes:

- Emotional fatigue
- Ongoing internal negotiation

- Restricted influence

Here, you're present but not fully expressed. This balancing act requires substantial energy.

3. Resist or Exit

This path involves action. You either challenge the system internally, escalate concerns to the highest possible level, or leave altogether. Sometimes, you may do all three.

Walking this path offers the following benefits:

- Alignment with personal values
- Clarity of position
- Potential to disrupt or expose

Of course, the costs are high and include:

- Increased risk
- Potential loss of stability
- Professional and personal consequences

As the most visible path, it's also the most demanding.

A Critical Truth

No path is inherently right. Every one of them is just aligned differently. What matters is not the path itself but whether the path reflects who you are, what you value, and what you're willing to carry.

Part II: A Framework for Decision

It can be dangerous to make reactive decisions in these environments. Instead, do your best to make informed, calculated choices.

Step 1: Assess the System

Ask the following:

- Are changes possible or are change efforts consistently avoided?

- Does leadership engage with dissent or redirect it?
- Is there any evidence of responsiveness?

Your answers must be based on what happens, not what is said or promised in private or public.

Step 2: Assess Your Position

Consider the following:

- Your exposure to risk
- Your level of influence
- Your proximity to decision-making

Every position carries differing amounts of leverage, and leverage matters.

Step 3: Assess Your Capacity

Be honest about the following:

- Emotional capacity
- Financial stability
- Professional flexibility

Keep in mind that you can't make all decisions at once, and that's okay. That's how reality works.

Step 4: Define Your Threshold

This is the most important step, during which you should ask yourself two vital questions.

- What am I willing to tolerate?
- What am I not willing to tolerate?

This helps you develop a defined threshold. Without one, the system will step in and define your threshold for you without your permission.

Step 5: Choose Intentionally

Do not choose what to do based on pressure, fear, or urgency. Instead, let clarity drive you forward, remembering that unclear decisions often lead to the following:

- Further entrenchment
- Regret
- Repetition

Part III: Path-Specific Guidance

Each path requires awareness, not assumption.

Stay and Assimilate

If you stay and assimilate, be honest with yourself. Acknowledge the trade-offs and maintain internal awareness. Monitor how your perspective shifts over time.

Alignment doesn't require blindness, but it does require acceptance.

Stay and Navigate

If you choose this path, be intentional. Set boundaries where possible and avoid complete disengagement. Maintain external perspective when possible.

Remember that survival without awareness leads to erosion, and awareness without boundaries leads to exhaustion.

Resist

Be prepared. Document carefully and build support intentionally. Understand the likely consequences of your resistance.

Exit

If you decide to make your escape, be deliberate, and plan before acting. You want to be led by clarity, not emotion and reaction.

As you leave, protect your narrative, since how you leave shapes how you process, rebuild, and move forward.

Part IV: The Truth About Choice

There is no perfect path, only paths paved with varying amounts of alignment. No decision eliminates cost. It simply redistributes it.

Many people struggle with that reality, because we want the safest option on the least disruptive path. We long for the decision with the least consequence to align with our personal values.

That option doesn't exist, at least not in controlling systems.

The Deeper Question

At some point, the system is removed from center stage, and you take its place. You begin to ask, "Who am I willing to be within or beyond the system?"

Because systems shape behavior, but they can only define identity if you allow them to do so.

Closing Reflection

Your choice will have a cost, no matter what. What cost are you willing to pay?

- The cost of silence?
- The cost of adaptation?
- The cost of resistance?
- The cost of change?

Each is real and valid, but only aligns with who you are and who you're becoming.

Micro-reflection

Which path are you currently on, and did you choose that path consciously?

What cost are you carrying right now?

What cost are you avoiding, and why?

Where does your current path align or conflict with your values?

What would it look like to make your next decision from clarity instead of pressure?

If nothing changes, who will you become by staying on your current path?

Chapter 16

DEPROGRAMMING AND HEALING: RECLAIMING CLARITY, IDENTITY, AND AGENCY

You don't leave a system unchanged. The work is learning what was shaped and deciding what you will keep.

Leaving or resisting a system doesn't end its impact, because the system doesn't just shape behavior. It shapes thought, perception, and identity, and none of these reset automatically. They linger in how you think, respond, and see yourself.

This indicates healing cannot be passive. It must be intentional.

Part I: Understanding What Happened

Before healing, there must be recognition of the system and its impact on you. Effects to look for include:

- Anticipating consequences that are no longer present
- Hesitating before speaking, even in safe spaces
- Second-guessing yourself more often

You may feel guarded and cautious, but remember—these

feelings aren't caused by weakness. They're caused by conditioning. Your mind adapted to an environment where expression carried risk, clarity was questioned, and reality was inconsistent.

Your brain is used to protecting you from harm and can't quit, even when protection is no longer needed.

Part II: The Residual Effects

The impact of these systems echo long after you leave.

1. **Cognitive Echoes**
   - Anticipating risk where none exists
   - Overanalyzing simple interactions
   - Searching for hidden meaning
2. **Emotional Residue**
   - Anger
   - Exhaustion
   - Frustration
   - Grief

     The grief you experience may be over many things, such as:
     - What you experienced
     - What you lost
     - What you expected your experience or impact to be
3. **Identity Disruption**
   - "Who was I before this?"
   - "Who am I now?"

Part III: Deprogramming (If You Stayed or Assimilated)

If you remained in the system or adapted to it, you may experience difficulty trusting your own judgment. You may develop a reflexive defense of authority and face dissent with discomfort.

Steps to Deprogram

1. **Reintroduce Questioning**
   Ask if your feelings make sense and believe the answer.
2. **Expose Yourself to Alternative Perspectives**
   Engage with people outside the system.
3. **Rebuild Internal Authority**
   Trust your observations again.
4. **Separate Identity from Role**
   Remember that who you are is not the system you were in.

Part IV: Healing (If You Resisted or Were Targeted)

Resisters often carry the weight that comes with impact. Common experiences include betrayal from others, loss of opportunity, isolation, and reputation damage. If you noticed a problem in the system and resisted it, those same problems are now knocking on your door.

Reputation Damage: The Invisible Injury

One of the most painful outcomes is not what happened but what gets said about you afterward.

It's not easy to be labeled as difficult, unaligned, or disruptive. Making things even worse is the fact that these labels can follow you.

Keep in mind that they're not the truth. They're made-up narratives that serve to keep the system alive and well.

Reputation Repair: Strategy

1. **Clarify Your Narrative**
   Remind yourself that you encountered a system that required alignment over integrity, and you chose not to compromise.

2. **Be Consistent, Not Reactive**
   Clarity builds credibility.
3. **Let Your Work Speak Again**
   Your actions will rebuild your reputation over time.
4. **Choose Strategic Disclosure**
   Not every space, family member, and hiring rep deserves your full story.

Reputation Healing: Internal Work

1. **Reject False Labels**
   You are not difficult. You are clear and principled.
2. **Find Your Anchors**
   Surround yourself with people who see you clearly.
3. **Rebuild Trust Gradually**
   Trust in yourself, others, and systems at your pace.

Part V: Healing from Rejection and Isolation

Rejection in these systems cuts deep, but rejection from a misaligned system is not a reflection of your value. It is often a reflection of your integrity, which the system cannot tolerate.

Part VI: Self-Care as Restoration

Healing requires intention. You must find rest, space, and safe connection that allows you to reflect without judgment.

You cannot rebuild while still operating in survival mode.

Part VII: Reclaiming Forward

Ask yourself the following:

- What will I tolerate now?
- What will I not tolerate?
- What does a healthy system look like to me?

- How do I ensure I do not lose myself again?

The Shared Truth

Whether you stayed, navigated, resisted, or left, you were shaped by the system. But you were not and are not defined by it.

Closing Reflection

The system may have influenced your behavior and disrupted your path, but it holds no claim on your identity or your future.

Once you understand what happened, you stop operating within the system and make choices that go beyond it.

Micro-reflection

What beliefs about yourself came from the system, and are they true?

What labels were placed on you, and do they belong to you?

Who are your anchors?

Where do you still feel hesitation, and why?

What would it look like to trust yourself again?

Chapter 17

THE EARLY YEARS

There was a time in my early career when I avoided conflict. I kept my head down and did my work. I learned where the lines were and took care not to step out of line.

I was, in many ways, a people pleaser.

I didn't challenge the status quo. Despite seeing obvious issues, I understood the risk. I was reliant on the income and building a career inside systems that didn't reward disruption.

In those spaces, I was often made to feel small, as though my contributions were less valuable. My perspective was not fully welcome, because alignment mattered more than insight.

So, I adjusted.

What I Saw

Over time, I saw the system more clearly.

I saw people get bullied for asking questions. I saw retaliation that was sometimes subtle, sometimes direct. I saw competent, effective individuals pushed out because they did not align. I saw cliques form and loyalty become currency. I saw environments where proximity to power created a different set of rules that could be bent, manipulated, or ignored entirely depending on who you were. I saw the most devoted individuals elevated beyond their skill set and experience.

And I saw the cost of this on teams, individuals, and outcomes.

The Shift

Clarity began to outweigh comfort as I gained experience and perspective. As I gained a growing recognition that staying silent was no longer neutral, the shift began.

Stepping Out on the Ledge

When I stepped out and decided to question the system, I was exposed and lonely. Trusted coworkers attempted to discredit and isolate me.

But I'd seen other people stand despite the cost. They chose integrity over comfort, clarity over alignment. They chose to act without knowing what the outcome would be.

And when one person stepped out, it created space. That space fueled me to take the same steps. It shifted something inside me, showing me that change is possible, even if that change means escape.

The Reality of the Trade-Off

Revolution comes with risk, fear, and potential retaliation. Rewards may be immediate, but many are delayed. The experience is layered, individualized, personal, and situational.

What I Ask of You

As you reflect on this book, don't choose a specific path. Ask yourself a few questions and answer them honestly.

- What am I seeing clearly now?
- What have I been adjusting to?
- What am I willing to tolerate?
- What am I unwilling to tolerate?

- What does alignment mean to me?
- How does my definition compare to the system's definition of alignment?
- Who do I want to be within or beyond this environment?

What Is Possible

You can have a thriving career that is not built on silence or blind alignment. You can have a thriving career grounded in courage, perseverance, humanity, compassion, and righteousness.

When present, these anchors shape your experience and the environments you help create.

Final Reflection

Systems will always exist. Some will be healthy, and some will not.

You can't always control the system you're in. You can, however, influence how you see and respond to the system and who you choose to become within it.

This book was written to make that choice clearer. Because once you see the system for what it is, you're no longer navigating blindly. You're deciding where, when, and how to navigate.

As you navigate, you are guided by awareness and the power to choose differently moving forward.

You were never the problem. You were the interruption. And now, you decide what comes next.

Appendix

VISUAL AIDS

You were never the problem. You were the interruption. And now, you are the one who gets to decide what comes next.

The Cycle of Control

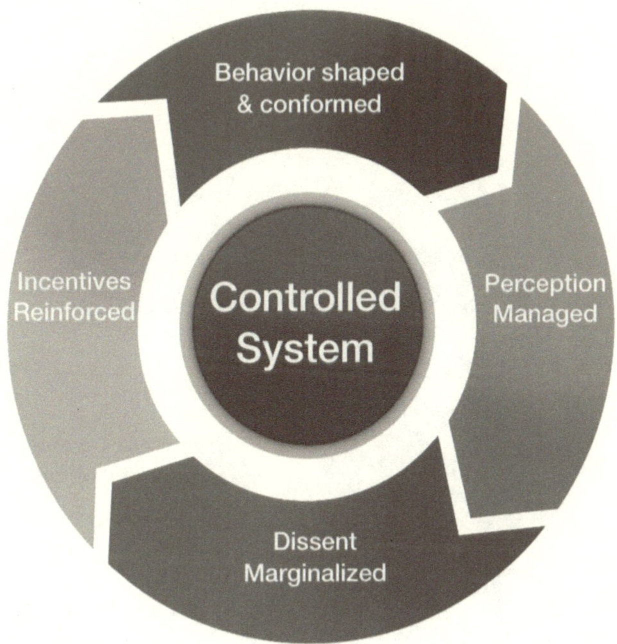

Adaptation → Acceptance → Dependence → Control

Decision Paths

Stay & Assimilate → Navigate & Resist → Exit & Leaave

Align & Conform | Observe & Challenge | Break & Move On

Who Do I Want to Be in This System??

Warning Signs & Red Flags

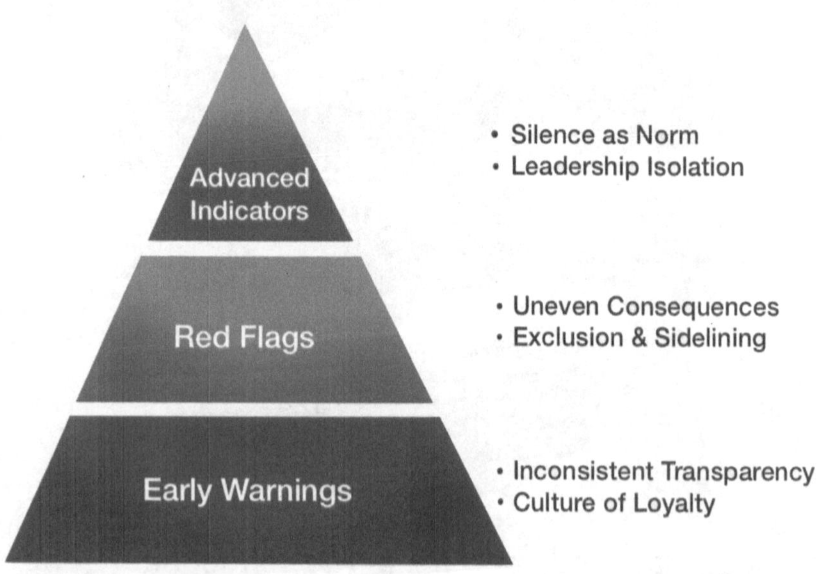

Steps to Rebuild the System

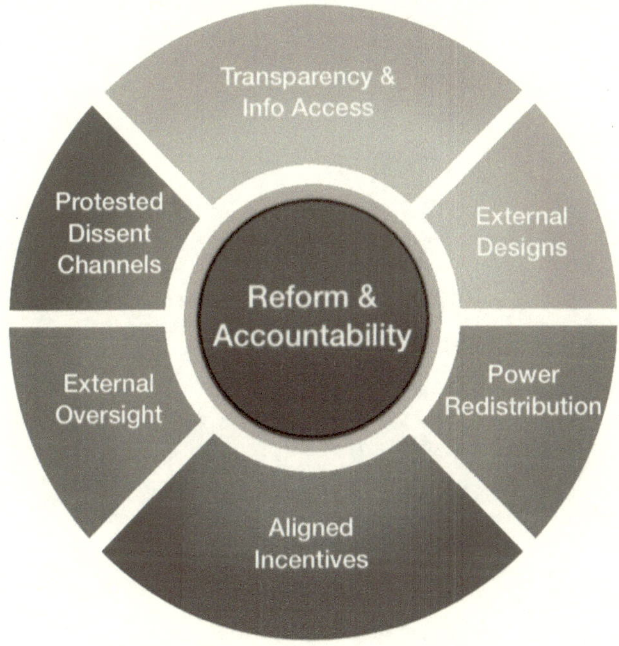

Disrupt Reform Rebuild

www.ingramcontent.com/pod-product-compliance
Lightning Source LLC
LaVergne TN
LVHW091105150826
845673LV00002B/728

9798891241701